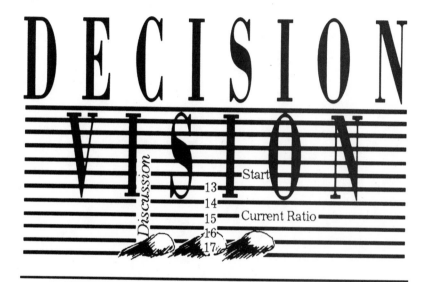

DECISION
VISION

Discussion

13
14
15
16
17

Start

Current Ratio

LEARNING TO MAKE CHOICES
WITH FOREVER IN MIND

GLORIA GAITHER

DECISION

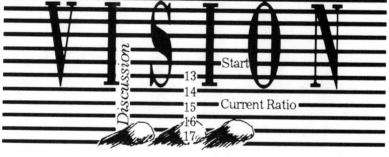

LEARNING TO MAKE CHOICES
WITH FOREVER IN MIND

Warner Press, Inc.
Anderson, Ind.

Published by
Warner Press, Inc.
Anderson, Indiana

All scripture passages, unless otherwise indicated, are from The Holy Bible,
New International Version. Copyright ©1973, 1978, 1984 International Bible
Society. Used by permission of Zondervan Bible Publishers.

Copyright ©1991 by Warner Press, Inc.
ISBN #0-87162-607-1   Stock #D3565
All Rights Reserved
Printed in the United States of America
Warner Press, Inc.

Arlo F. Newell, Editor in Chief
Dan Harman, Book Editor
Cover by Larry Lawson and Debbie Apple

When the first edition of this book was published, Bill and I felt there was real need for helpful biblical directives for making choices. We could never have imagined that less than a decade later persons of the 1990s would be living at such an accelerated pace that even little children would be developing ulcers from stress! Never before have human beings been so bombarded by so many complex decisions! Children, teenagers, college students, young upwardly mobile adults, executives, home builders, adults entering second and third vocations—all of us—desperately need trustworthy directions for making choices—choices that will effect the rest of our lives!

We need illumination . . .

We need insight . . .

We need clear vision . . .

. . . so that we can make decisions that have some "eternity" in them.

The timeless eternal priorities of God's Word are the only reliable guidelines for such a whirlwind time. It is for this reason that Warner Press felt it was time to republish the principles Bill and I have learned from God's Word for making choices in a changing world.

—Gloria Gaither

Contents

Acknowledgments

This book would never have been written had not some special people made decisions that affected my life and this project. My thanks to

My mother, Dorothy Sickal, who decided to have a second child and to listen to a lifetime of words and ideas from that daughter;

My children, who have encouraged me to write and pursue my education, even when it meant sacrifice on their part;

Phyllis, who deciphered my handwriting to prepare the original manuscript, and my assistant Deborah for seeing to so many details;

All the people who shared their personal decision-making experiences with me and gave their permission for these stories to be used;

And Bill, whose idea this book was in the first place.

Foreword

The whole world is watching! Time was when the "evangelical Christian community" was considered an insignificant subculture from "across the tracks." Sometimes scorned, sometimes joked about, often dismissed, and seldom taken seriously by the secular world, the "company of the committed" was left to the lonely task of salting the earth.

But now, thanks to the publicity given the "born-again" label by the media, professed Christians in the White House, the emergence of political clout in the form of politically active Christian groups, and the unavoidable visibility of the "electronic church," the so-called Jesus movement of the sixties has moved into the mainstream. Surveys report sixty to eighty percent of the American population claiming a "born-again" spiritual experience, while evangelists credit conservative theology with the shift to a more politically conservative tone in the country.

It would seem that the candle has indeed moved from under the bushel to atop the candlestick. The larger question is, Now that the world is watching, what does it see?

Probably nothing hurts the cause of Christ more than one who claims His name but consistently makes decisions that are contrary to the very intent and spirit of His Word. Our daily decision making says far more to the non-Christian world than all of the verbal, personal testimonies we might share. There's a current saying, "walk your talk." It is very simple, but it makes the point—our lives, as reflected in our decision making, must be consistent with what we profess to be as Christians. I want to say quickly that Gloria and I do not believe in easy answers for hard problems, but in our thirty years together we have tried carefully to make rational decisions—regarding our personal lives, our family, our ministry, and our daily business responsibilities—based on the Bible and how it continues to reveal itself to us.

I am probably prejudiced, but I really feel as though Gloria has been able, in this book, to draw out some of the principles that we have learned in our daily decision making, and I am excited about the possibility of sharing these guidelines with those of you who read this book.

Personal Note

When I first met my husband Bill, both of us were high school English teachers. Bill had written a few songs that he had sung with his brother and sister in area churches and had introduced to the church choir he directed. At the time, we planned to go on teaching and to live a fairly simple life, but soon after our marriage we began writing songs together. God was teaching us so much, and we felt we just had to find a way to express the things that were so meaningful in our lives.

Gradually, others started singing our songs (friends like Doug Oldham—and the Imperials, and the Speer Family). We found ourselves devoting more and more of our time to writing, singing (as the Bill Gaither Trio), and publishing. Soon there wasn't enough time to divide between teaching and music, so we had to choose between the two things we loved so much.

We resigned our teaching positions and chose to devote full time to communicating the gospel that had made our lives so full and complete. About this time our first child was born. As our family, our businesses, and our ministry grew, our decisions began to affect not just our own lives, but the lives of other people as well—our children, our extended family, our associates, our business partners, our employees, teachers, the community, our public audiences, and those reached by our work through radio and television, recordings, and print. We felt excited that our ideas were finding wide exposure, but we also began to realize that "everyone to whom much is given, of him will much be required" (Luke 12:48, RSV).

Personal Note

Not only did we discover that decisions we made were becoming far-reaching; we also became aware that they were growing more complex. Often we found that easy, one-issue answers were not enough. Situations were not always black-and-white, open-and-shut. There were many complicated aspects to consider. Simplistic solutions would not work. We came to see that at times a solution might be positive in some ways and damaging in others. There were situations in which a surface, obvious decision might soothe matters over for the moment, only to erupt later with hurtful and damaging results. Or, on the other hand, there were occasions when what seemed to be a painful solution brought creative and positive results later on, because it was the right thing to do—not easy, but right.

Actually, it was Bill's idea for me to write this book, and it came out of some needs we have had in our own lives. When we were beginning our pilgrimage, we would have found useful some practical help in formulating a decision-making strategy. Most of the things I've written about here we have had to learn for ourselves; thank God for His Word and the prayers and counsel of wise friends who loved us!

This is not an "easy answers for hard questions" book. It isn't a "how to" book. Rather, it is a collection of guidelines we have found helpful in our own lives as we have tried to "work out our own salvation with fear and trembling." Perhaps it is more accurately a do-it-yourself kit. If it is to be helpful to you, you will have to make it work in your own situation.

The "rules," if you want to call them that, are based on God's Word, the only trustworthy measuring stick for anything in our lives. These guidelines have been helpful to me, and I hope they will help you, too, as you work to become more effectively God's person in the daily decision-making process.

Gloria Gaither

1

To Live Is to Decide

Above all else, guard your heart, for it is the wellspring of life.
—Proverbs 4:23, NIV

I found him on the stairway—on the seventh step—
huddled up close to the wall, looking very small in
just his underwear. (Our two-year-old son was always
happiest in his underwear, and we would laugh about
the way he always left a trail of clothes from the back
door whenever he had been somewhere in his "stiff ol'
dress-up clothes.") But he wasn't happy now—not
even in his favorite attire.

"Look at me!" he said, his little face all serious and
scared.

"Look at me! I'm shrinking!"

An hour ago he'd been excited about the party we
would have with lots of relatives and neighborhood
children. He had helped me make the plans, set the
table, line up the hats and noisemakers, and ice the
cake. But when the doorbell rang and I said, "Go let
them in!" he ran and hid. My timid little helper just
couldn't quite face up to a big title like *host*.

DECISION VISION

Our son wasn't the first person to feel himself "shrinking" when faced with the demands of life. There have been times when I, too, have felt myself too small in the face of real situations and wanted to run away. I suspect all of us at times have felt like hiding from problems and obligations and decisions.

But life won't let us escape. Obstacles and problems make up the warp in the fabric of our days, and across that warp we weave the threads of our decisions. The problems we face, the choices we make—these create the unique design of our lives.

Chances are, every one of you who holds this book in your hand is facing some decision. We all deal with issues that demand answers. Every day, we find ourselves having to make decisions, and most of the time the choices don't seem to be very "spiritual" or even important. This, at least, is true for me. Most days, moreover, I find the choices come hurling themselves at me so fast there isn't even time to philosophize about them.

Some decisions are so simple they seem almost automatic: which blouse to wear with my burgundy tweed skirt . . . which brand of toothpaste to buy . . . which route to take to the shopping center or the office. Other choices that seem simple may be actually more complicated. Can I really afford to buy this suit when so many people in the world woke up hungry this morning? Am I being brainwashed by that TV commercial for a jazzy sports car, or will a smaller, less expensive car do just as well? Should our family spend a long weekend together at the resort on the lake, or should we put the money in the bank for an emergency? Questions about my work, my children, my home, and my relationships march like an army through the course of my days—and many of these are questions that seem to defy easy answers.

Time was when society itself gave us some direction in decision making. Most people subscribed to a basic moral code that defined, at least, what society expected. In my grandparents' day, it was generally agreed that "good" people would pay their bills, never cheat a neighbor, tell the truth, be faithful to their spouses, and support their families. Most people built their social life around the church and the community and took pride in supporting both.

But today situations are different. Society—the family, the school, the government—seems to have abdicated its role of moral leadership. Even many churches have lost the will to define direction for us. Today we find ourselves feeling alone and perplexed. Shifting values and confusing social changes have shaken the foundations from beneath our feet while external and internal pressures build up around and in us. Many of us find it increasingly difficult to get our bearings.

Dr. Frederic Flach, Associate Clinical Professor of Psychiatry at Cornell University Medical College, describes our disorientation in this way: "When there is no common ethic—when the various segments of society cannot agree on a few definitive rights and wrongs—the resulting ambiguity leaves every individual highly vulnerable to every new formula that seems to offer relief from distress and anxiety or a new kind of joy that is generally rather ill-defined. Worse yet, when there is little consensus about what is best for the individual or for society, there is a strong tendency to resort to the rule of force. 'What's in it for me?' has become a common yardstick, with manipulation and abuse so much the norm that we have even developed schools of psychological self-defense, such as systematic assertive therapy, to protect ourselves."[1]

The ambiguity in our society has prompted many people to turn to leaders who promise to solve their problems for them. Social scientists tell us that it is, in fact, just such a feeling of rootlessness and lack of direction that has given rise to so many new cults and the popularity of certain authoritarian figures. It is

frightening to see our young people being influenced—
even hypnotized—into following sick philosophies,
simply because those philosophies offer them *some*
answer. Cultism is, of course, a coward's way out, a
way that ultimately leads to mindlessness, but in a
time of chaos it can seem an attractive solution.

Most of us at times would feel relieved to find a
nice, neat set of rules or guidelines to which we could
refer, a sort of foolproof list of easy answers for hard
questions. That way we wouldn't have to struggle
with our choices. As Gwendolyn Brooks writes:

> People like definite decisions,
> Tidy answers, all the little ravellings
> Snipped off, the lint removed, they
> Hop happily among the roughs,
> Calling what they can't clutch insanity
> Or saintliness.[2]

But there are no easy answers. Whether we like it
or not, we are continually faced with the ultimate
question of whom we will serve and, beyond that
primary choice, with countless daily decisions. No
laws, no pat answers, will save us from the responsibility or the destiny of being decision makers, and no
human-made system could ever be adequate to cover
the complicated choices we face.

Now, if we were to be influenced by a society
around us that has largely come to accept, as its
operating philosophy, existential nihilism—the belief
that we have come by accident into our human condition and that we ultimately are going nowhere—we
might ask ourselves, "Why do choices make any difference?" Everywhere we turn—in everyday conversation, in printed material, on television and radio—we
are bombarded by the do-your-own-thing, whatever-
turns-you-on outlook. And indeed, if human beings
were only sophisticated animals who evolved by acci-

dent on a dying planet, if nothing were eternal, if there were no God and life were only a one-way trip from nothingness to nothingness, then we might rightly feel that our decisions wouldn't matter. Other than merely minimizing the pain and despair of our meaningless existence, moral codes would be pointless. One choice would be as good as another, for "good" and "bad" would have no meaning beyond the convenience of the moment.

But I do not accept that operating philosophy. I am a Christian. I am concerned about decision making because I believe our choices *do* matter, not just for today or the present moment, but forever. I believe, in fact, that as a Christian I have the responsibility and joy in life to become more and more aware of the "eternity" in each moment. Because I have chosen to follow Christ, my aim is to learn to recognize and spend my life on things that will last forever.

I have come to believe that "eternal life" is not just a promised reward that we will have in the sweet by and by, but a dimension our lives can have right now. I believe that Jesus Christ came to show us God's value system more clearly, so that we could learn how to make new kinds of choices—choices with "eternity" in them. The more we learn to live with a "forever" view, the more we are released from the stranglehold of pessimism and materialism. The despair of spending the energies of our whole lives on a terminal course is traded for the joy that comes from being convinced that we do ultimately matter and that we can choose to invest in things that will not die.

As a Christian, then, I believe individual decisions make a difference. I also believe that being a Christian changes the process by which decisions are made. Our task as Christians is somehow to get our beliefs out of the realm of rhetoric and stained glass and into the nitty gritty of our day-to-day living—the daily process of decision making. And I believe Jesus has given us the key for doing this.

Jesus knew that not enough laws could ever be written to give us all the answers. He knew that in a constantly changing world no one code could cover all the decisions we would face—how could laws be written in His day that would speak to our modern age with its high-speed travel, instant satellite-relayed information, drug culture, moral ambiguity, international high finance, and constantly changing lifestyles? He also knew that laws of themselves would not be enough to control our lives and decisions— simply because it just wouldn't be possible for us on our own to keep all the laws. As Paul says in Romans 7, "We know that the law is spiritual; but I am unspiritual. . . . For what I want to do I do not do, but what I hate I do. . . . When I want to do good, evil is right there with me" (vv. 14, 15, 21, NIV).

Yet Jesus dared to say that he had the answer. In two sentences He gave us all the law we would need for all time. "Love the Lord your God with all your heart, and with all your soul, and with all your mind," He said (Matt. 22:37 RSV), and "Love your neighbor as much as you love yourself" (v. 39, Living Bible). If we truly obey these two laws, He tells us, we won't need any others.

When the respectable leaders, the keepers of the law, brought to Jesus the woman caught in the very act of adultery and threw her like a sack of garbage at His feet, He did not initiate a cerebral and theological debate about society's laws governing sexual behavior. Obviously, the woman had broken those laws. Anyone could see she had made some seriously wrong choices. Instead, Jesus stooped down and began to write in the same dust in which the woman cowered terrified at the feet of her accusers. Then He stood and spoke to them: "He that is without sin among you, let him first cast a stone at her."

We don't know what Jesus wrote in the dust, but

we do know that what He did and what He said shot like an arrow straight to the souls of her accusers, revealing to them secret, hidden sins of motive and attitude—the kind of sins that few can see on the outside but that are glaringly clear to God. His words made them drop their judgmental murder weapons and slink away into the shadows.

When they were all gone, Jesus said to the woman, "Who accuses you?" (my paraphrase). She looked up, her frightened eyes darting about in search of those who had arrested her. They were not there. Timidly, she answered Jesus. Her answer was almost a question, for she knew that, according to the law, she deserved to face the death penalty. "No man, Lord." The recognition of who she was and who He was, was all there in that one word: *Lord*. She could never be the same again.

"I don't accuse you, either," said Jesus. He told her to go her way, and to live up to what she had come to know with her heart: "Go, and sin no more."

In Jesus' words we, too, begin to find the secret of restructuring our own lives in a chaotic world. Jesus understood the soul of man and knew that right choices could never be legislated. We can't become "good" from the outside in, but only from the inside out. He introduced a revolutionary idea: *the heart can be changed*—MUST be changed. When the motivation is healed and purified, the resulting action will reflect that wholeness.

Jesus assured us that when our priorities are aligned with His eternal value system, the specific choices we face will come more clearly into focus as well. This same eternal view caused Jesus himself to choose to go to the cross, and it was from that cross that He said of His own accusers, "Father, forgive them; for they know not what they do." He was expressing His sadness, not over what his executioners were doing to his physical body, but over what they were doing to

15

themselves—to the part of themselves that was eternal. With those words and that cross He punctuated history with an exclamation mark to finish the sentence that was the theme of His message: "A new law I give you . . . LOVE!" Love in us could give us the power to make choices that otherwise we would be too weak to make.

Jesus knew that law alone cannot force us to a decision to be truthful when we find ourselves in a compromising position. But He also knew that if we genuinely love another person we will not say things that will damage character. A law against theft will not rid the world of stealing, but a love that roots out covetousness will. Enforcing laws against murder and adultery is difficult. But if our hearts were to be filled with a love that empties our lives of lust, bitterness, and hate, such laws would be superfluous.

How thankful we should be that He lived and died to show us a better way! If there had to be a law to govern every situation in our lives that demands a decision, we would find ourselves so bogged down and oppressed that we couldn't make any decision. Our minds and nervous systems would be short-circuited from the gigantic moral overload. But the cross of Christ made possible a new foundation for making right decisions—the purification of our hearts, the re-creation of what we *are*.

C. S. Lewis once said, "No clever arrangements of bad eggs ever made a good omelette." What we truly are will dictate our choices, no matter how we try to camouflage or hide it, and no amount of moral effort will make us choose rightly if our hearts aren't right. Sooner or later the pressures and pace of our lives will expose what we really are. The writer of Proverbs wisely puts it this way, "Keep thy heart with all diligence; for out of it are the issues of life" (4:23).

Morality would be a cumbersome burden if each decision of our lives had to be carefully checked against some itemized, written code. We would be in constant turmoil worrying about whether some code was overlooked or misinterpreted. The joy of right living would be strangled in legalism. But it is exactly this sort of system that was in effect before Jesus brought the renovation of the human heart and motives through His death and resurrection and then provided us with the live-in support of the Holy Spirit.

"The letter killeth, but the spirit giveth life" (2 Cor. 3:6) is more than a religious axiom! Good choices come most freely from the purist possible motives; these come from a heart repossessed by the transforming power of love. Love does what law could never do.

When it comes to lessons about living and loving, the family circle has been for me a fine schoolroom, and our children have often been the teachers. So it is not surprising that my kitchen was the setting for a recent refresher course on law and love.

At our house a favorite breakfast treat for the kids was cinnamon rolls—you know, the kind that comes in a cardboard tube that you whack on the corner of the cabinet, the kind with cinnamon and brown sugar sprinkled all over the top of each circle of dough, the kind that comes with a little white container of gooey icing to spread on when the rolls are all brown and hot. Also, at our house, everyone's favorite cinnamon roll was the "middle one," because it was soft and chewy all the way around with no crusty edges. Usually, the first person dressed and down to the kitchen was the first person to "call it," and that was usually Benjy, our youngest. Oh, sometimes it was his big sister Suzanne, but it was almost never Amy, our middle daughter, because Amy was our slowest morning mover.

One cold winter morning I fixed cinnamon rolls, and Benjy smelled their sweet, spicy aroma filling the house. Sure enough he was the first one down and the first to "call it," "I get the middle one!" he yelled as he bounded into the kitchen and sniffed his way toward the oven where I was lifting out the rolls.

"Benjy," I answered. "I know you called it first and that's our rule, but, you know, it's been a long time since Amy has had the middle one. How about letting her have it this time?" He thought a while as I started icing one outside roll.

"Well, okay," he said reluctantly, "but let's not ice the middle one!" Seeing me look a little hesitant, he begged, "Aw com'on, Mom. It's just a joke. Let's see what she'll do!"

I saved back the icing for the middle roll and put the rest on the table. As usual, Amy was the last one in her seat. Benjy asked a *short* blessing then shoved the pan of rolls under Amy's nose. "Here, Amy, you can have the middle one."

She took it, but didn't seem to notice what we had done. Benjy squirmed a little in his chair, then announced very loudly, "I think I'll take this one. It has *lots* of icing!"

Still no response from Amy.

"Yum!" said Benjy, licking one finger, "this icing sure tastes good!"

Still nothing.

Finally, I couldn't stand the suspense any longer. "Amy," I said, "Did you notice we played a little trick on you? Your roll doesn't have any icing."

"I know, Mom. It's okay. I just thought there wasn't enough to go around."

Well, she sure did ruin our joke, but she also started our day with a gently powerful statement: When love is the law, we need no other.

FOR WORK AND DISCUSSION

Ask yourself these questions:

1. Am I willing to take the responsibility of being a decision maker?

   a. Think of times when, in one way or another, you "ran away" from decisions. How did you feel? Why did deciding seem so difficult?

   b. What are some ways we as adults "run away" from choices?

2. Do I expect my family, my church, or the laws of the land to give me "easy answers?"

   a. Can you remember times when a choice might have been "lawful" but not expedient?

   b. Can you think of times when you might have been right in fact but wrong in attitude? What is legalism?

3. Am I being realistic right now? What decisions do I know in my heart that I must face and make soon?

---

1. Fredric Flach, *Choices: Coping with Personal Changes* (Philadelphia: J. B. Lippincott, 1977).
2. Gwendolyn Brooks, "Memorial to Ed Bland" in *Annie Allen*. L. B. Fischer Company, 1945. ©1945 by Gwendolyn Brooks Blakely. Reprinted by permission of Harper & Row, Publishers, Inc.

2

Where Do I Want to Go?

Show me thy ways, O Lord; teach me thy paths. Lead me in thy truth, and teach me: for thou art the God of my salvation.
—*Psalm 25:4-5*

T he cat only grinned when he saw Alice. It looked good-natured, she thought: still it had very long claws and a great many teeth, so she felt that it ought to be treated with respect.

"Cheshire-Puss," she began, rather timidly, as she did not at all know whether it would like the name; however, it only grinned a little wider, "Come, it's pleased so far," thought Alice, and she went on. "Would you tell me please which way I ought to go from here?"

"That depends a good deal on where you want to get to," said the Cat.

"I don't much care where—" said Alice.

"Then it doesn't matter which way you go," said the Cat.[1]

If, like Alice in Wonderland, you don't much care where you're going, then, as the Cheshire Cat said, "It doesn't make any difference which way you go." But if you do care about where you are going, then the road you take makes all the difference in the world. It is a fallacy that "all roads lead to the same place." We would think that sort of advice idiocy if we were asking directions to San Francisco or Chicago. It is just as absurd when we are seeking direction for our lives.

Whether we are sizing up our lives in total or confronting a specific decision, our important first questions must be, "Where do I want to go?" "What are my objectives?" "What, ultimately, do I want to accomplish?"

Identifying our objectives can be a complex task. Often there is more than one objective. For the Christian, the ultimate objective might be to best serve God with our abilities and talents, or to become more like Jesus. These are long-range objectives, and they are of prime importance. Added to them may be other, short-term goals: to house or care for our families, to be good stewards of our finances, to finish a specific project or to mend a broken relationship.

But why is recognizing and defining our goals so important? In the first place, it helps keep us honest with ourselves about what our real priorities are. Whether we want to admit it or not, all our choices ultimately will be dictated by what we really want: *the strongest want will win.* We human beings can be very clever at conning ourselves. We can rationalize—even spiritualize—almost anything. But, in the final analysis, what we think is most important is what we will choose, no matter what we tell ourselves or other people.

I may say, for example, that I can't help with a project at church because I don't have time. In reality I may be saying: "Spending my time in that way is not as important to me as spending my time having coffee with my neighbor." When I say I can't afford to give more than my tithe, I may be saying: "I believe that putting my money in new furniture is more important than sending money to the Middle East."

Now, there may be nothing wrong with buying furniture, and having coffee with a neighbor may actually be a better use of my time than making crocheted doilies for the church bazaar. The important thing is that taking the time to recognize my true priorities and goals helps me be honest with myself about what I believe is really important.

This, in turn, can help me recognize activities of mine that may be working against my real goals. Shakespeare, in *The Rape of Lucrece*, said, "[Who] sells eternity to get a toy?/For one sweet grape who will the vine destroy?" Jesus said it another way: "For what is a man profited, if he shall gain the whole world, and lose his own soul?" (Matt. 16:26). We all recognize how crazy it would be to trade eternity for a fickle momentary pleasure. Yet most of us can think of times when we did just that in little ways by choices we made about our time, energies, money, and abilities. Taking time to define our goals and objectives can help us avoid such waste.

Deciding where we want to go can also keep us from making costly mistakes. A friend of mine who is a contractor recently told me that one of the biggest problems with which he has to deal is indecision. The following story is reenacted over and over in his business.

A couple whom we shall call Dick and Helen wanted to build a house. They hired a contractor and an architect. At the first meeting with the architect, Dick and Helen began by telling him all of the things they had admired in other houses they had seen. They showed him pictures of a Tudor-style house they thought attractive, and suggested several things they might need—like a two-car garage and a master bedroom on the ground floor, a workshop for Dick's woodworking hobby, and a sewing room for Helen.

DECISION VISION

The architect drew up the plans according to what had been suggested and scheduled a time to meet again. When the time came for this meeting, however, Helen had seen another house she liked that had a large picture window in the dining room and a fireplace in the den. Dick had decided that his woodworking area should not be a part of the basement, but should instead be in the garage. The architect made these changes, for which, of course, there was an added fee.

The plans were approved and the contractor started to build. When the framework and ceiling joists were in place, Dick decided that he would rather the garage and workshop not be attached to the house; he wanted a separate unit with its own heating and cooling system. Making this change required disassembling the attached garage framework, pouring a new cement slab for the garage, and restructuring an inside wall to become a supporting outside wall.

Throughout the building process, this story was repeated. Time after time, Dick and Helen made changes in their plans. Before the project was completed, costly changes and delays ate up their life's savings; they were forced to abandon construction. The house still stands half-finished on the outskirts of town, because Dick and Helen lacked a clear objective and therefore destroyed their dream by changing direction too many times.

You may be thinking that most of our daily decisions aren't as big as those Dick and Helen faced, or the results so drastic. But as important as it may seem, this couple was only building a house; you and I are constructing lives! We are making decisions about that kind of building every day. Houses aren't "forever," but people are! Dick's and Helen's dream was to make something of mortar and bricks, but if we lose sight of our true objectives and forfeit our dreams, the outcome could be infinitely more serious. That makes the

steps we take along the paths we choose very important.

It must be universally true that high school students
hate to memorize poetry. But teachers, like doctors,
go on insisting that we do things, not necessarily
because we like them, but because they are good for
us. It was some such dubious rationale that motivated
me to require that my junior-year English students
master several lines by Robert Frost. (A few—about
the same percentage as Jesus got when he healed the
lepers—have even returned during those intervening
years to thank me!)

Some of those lines were a poem called "The Road
Not Taken," which goes like this:

> Two roads diverged in a yellow wood,
> And sorry I could not travel both
> And be one traveler, long I stood
> And looked down one as far as I could
> To where it bent in the undergrowth;
>
> Then took the other, as just as fair,
> And having perhaps the better claim,
> Because it was grassy and wanted wear;
> Though as for that the passing there
> Has worn them really about the same,
>
> And both that morning equally lay
> In leaves no step had trodden black.
> Oh, I kept the first for another day!
> Yet knowing how way leads on to way,
> I doubted if I would ever come back.
>
> I shall be telling this with a sigh
> Somewhere ages and ages hence:
> Two roads diverged in a wood, and I—
> I took the one less traveled by,
> And that has made all the difference.[2]

DECISION VISION

This poem dramatically illustrates several truths about decision making that I think are important. One is that we *do* have to make decisions—unless we just want to sit in the middle of life's road and rot! Another is that we cannot let the crowd do our choosing for us; the well-worn path of the pack is not necessarily the best one for us. Many times the Christian decision maker finds himself taking the way that "was grassy and wanted wear," while the majority that does not share the Christian's objectives take the more traveled road. Many great men and women—people like Ruth, John the Baptist, the prophets, Martin Luther, John and Charles Wesley, Susan B. Anthony, Martin Luther King, Mother Teresa, Thomas Paine, and Abraham Lincoln—have found the paths they chose to be lonely ones.

But one of the most interesting things "The Road Not Taken" shows about decision making is that, in the choices we face, the alternatives often seem to be equal, just as the paths the poet faced in the forest looked more or less alike. At the time, we may feel that it really doesn't matter which way we choose. Both paths seem harmless; either decision seems acceptable. Without much in-depth thinking—and without determining ahead of time where we eventually want to go—we may choose the one we like best and move ahead. Nothing jumps out to grab us. Nothing awful happens, so we feel safe and almost wonder if people don't make too much of being so conscientious. But all the same, we may be going the wrong way!

One morning we were reading the creation story in Genesis to our children before they left for school, and afterward talked together about the way Eve used just this sort of reasoning. God had told Adam and Eve that they would die if they ate of the forbidden fruit, but the serpent said to Eve, "Aw, go ahead, You won't die." And sure enough, she didn't drop dead when she took a bite. What Eve didn't realize was that what Satan meant by "die" was immediate, simplistic. What God meant by "die" was far-reaching, multidimensional, and eternal. The fruit *looked* as good as other fruit; it tasted good. So, using her short-sighted evidence, Eve went to Adam with her new discovery.

So often we say to teen-agers, "Don't do that; it will harm you." What they often don't see or hear is the dimension to the word *harm*. So they try drugs and find that the horror stories they have heard about "bad trips" don't happen to them. Or they enter into casual sexual relationships, endorsing the philosophy that it's nobody's business as long as "no one gets hurt." They cheat on exams and don't get caught or lie to their parents, who never suspect. But the "harm" is being done just the same, and the damage is to things that are far more important than physical health or reputation. What is being destroyed is trust, self-respect, integrity, and the ability to enjoy simple things; the injury is spiritual and emotional, and it gouges deep into the very sinews of life. Seemingly inconsequential decisions can have serious consequences in the long run.

In "The Road Not Taken," Frost doesn't say exactly why he chose the path he did. Something inside him— perhaps some long-held goals, some ideas about where he really wanted to go—urged him to choose the less-traveled road. At the time, he told himself that perhaps someday he would come back and try the other path, too. Yet, knowing human nature, he felt deep inside that that plan would never materialize.

In our lives, far-reaching choices are often made without fanfare. In fact, we may look back and realize only in hindsight that one day we stood at a fork in the road. Someone has said, "People's lives turn on small hinges. People make many decisions, some of seemingly little consequence, but the total of these decisions determine the happiness or misery of their lives."

DECISION VISION

Agnes de Mille, the famous American choreographer, wrote in her book *Dance to the Piper*, "No trumpets sound when the important decisions of our life are made. Destiny is made known silently."[3] Great destinies so often hang on the thread of a seemingly small choice that I am coming to believe there are no "small" decisions. Looking back over the past, most of us can see where our lives took certain, even dramatic, changes in direction because of a "small" decision.

I can think of several such life-changing decisions in my life. At the time, the choices seemed not to be so important, and the alternatives seemed quite equal. One such decision was the choice of a college.

I thought at the time that the important choice was whether or not to go to college. Where I would go seemed quite unimportant. I had received scholarships to two, and the chance of one at another that offered an outstanding speech and forensics department. The sensible choice seemed to be the school where I would get the most financial aid; my parents' budget was limited, and I knew they couldn't help me much. Earning my degree from an academically prestigious school seemed attractive. Yet, in the end, I chose to attend a small Christian liberal arts college where the financial aid was not as adequate. That choice as much as any other has since shaped the direction of my life, because while attending that college I chose my life's companion. It was also at that school, perhaps because it was a small, caring, community that my life was deeply affected by specific professors who took the time to help me identify and develop my special gifts. Because of opportunities afforded me by that particular institution, I was called upon to develop a wide range of work skills.

Other choices have affected my life profoundly. There have been decisions to try one more time to mend a broken relationship, to say yes to a difficult assignment, to lay aside some "necessary" work to be with my children, or to visit someone almost forgotten.

There have been failures, too—things left undone until it was too late, words I wish I had said, choices that hurt others, or opportunities I let slip through my fingers. Decisions tend to be progressive; they build on one another. Often single decisions that seem so insignificant are, in reality, ever-so-gradual steps in an ultimate direction.

So often we see only the surface and the immediate and ignore the deep and long-range result—entertaining a "harmless" thought, bending the truth, rationalizing a weakness, keeping something that doesn't belong to us because it is "worthless anyway" or we "had it coming." Deep pits are begun with a single shovelful of dirt, and mountains are climbed one step at a time. As we face those "small" decisions that may change the course of our lives, having our goals and objectives defined can help keep us going in the right direction.

Of course, clarifying our objectives doesn't guarantee that we'll always make the right decisions. At times choosing between two seemingly equal possibilities seems impossible for us. And there are times when our objectives seem to conflict. For instance, today I must ask myself: "Do I stay at my desk and work until five o'clock, or do I quit at two (even though I may lose my train of thought), so I can be home to spend some of my day with my daughter?" I want to be a good mother, one who isn't so busy doing "good" things that she misses important fleeting moments. But I also feel that God has called and equipped me to communicate life-changing ideas. These conflicting objectives both result from my higher objective of wanting to invest my time and energies in the best way I can in the light of eternal values. Both are good goals. How do I decide?

On our own, in situations like that, we may be

unable to choose wisely which path to take. But as Christians we are not on our own! We have the resources of God's wisdom to help us choose from the alternatives we face, and to help us decide on goals and objectives that fit in with His plan for us.

God has promised His help and guidance in all our decisions—big and little. We need to face every fork in life's road with the prayer of the psalmist on our lips: "Search me, O God, and know my heart; test my thoughts. Point out anything you find in me that makes you sad, and lead me along the path of everlasting life" (Ps. 139:23-24, Living Bible).

FOR WORK AND DISCUSSION

1. Make a list of the long-range and primary objectives in your life. State them as honestly as you can.

2. List the specific decisions you now are facing.

3. Now list the goals that relate to each particular decision.

4. Compare your primary goals with the specific goals. Check any that may be in conflict. What steps would you need to take to maintain and achieve your primary objectives in this situation? Will any of your short-range goals have to be changed or abandoned if your long-range goals are to be reached?

5. Think of conditions in your life right now that seem insignificant, yet that, with careful observation, you can recognize as subtle choices of a basic direction. Are these "small" choices taking you where you ultimately want to go? Examples: credit buying; Bible-study and prayer habits; social drinking; budgeting of time; attention to hobbies, sports, or pastimes; language patterns; attitudes toward the hungry, disadvantaged, or oppressed; attitudes toward your role as a citizen of your country, and so forth.

Where Do I Want to Go?

6. Can you think of areas in your life in which you are allowing others, overtly or subtly, to make your choices for you?

1. Lewis Carroll, *Alice's Adventures in Wonderland* (Cleveland: World Publishing Co., 1946), 80.
2. Edward Connery Lathem, ed., *The Poetry of Robert Frost*. 1944 by Robert Frost, 1969 by Holt, Rinehart, and Winston. Used by permission of Holt, Rinehart, and Winston, Publishers.
3. Agnes De Mille, *Dance to the Piper* (Boston: Little, Brown & Co., 1951), 77.

3

God's Word and Our Decisions

The whole Bible was given to us by inspiration from God and is useful to teach us what is true and to make us realize what is wrong in our lives; it straightens us out and helps us do what is right. —2 *Timothy 3:16, Living Bible*

How can I tell you how important the Word of God has become to me in making decisions? How can the words I choose make you know, as I have come to know, that this book we call the Bible is a living, breathing organism capable of reaching into the very core of our days and touching us with wisdom and guidance for every problem we face?

So often, when I walk into troubled homes, I see the Bible, dusty and neglected, on some hard-to-reach shelf. And I want to shout or cry—or whisper—"There! There is the answer you long so much to find. It's buried there with dozens of other books. Don't you see? It's not just another book. It is *Life!*"

When I was a little girl, I remember times when I would rush in from school and throw my books down on the table as kids will do. Once in a while they would land on top of the Bible, which stayed on the table (where our family gathered for all kinds of food). Mother would always walk over and pick up my books. "Don't lay them on the Bible, dear," she would say. There was a tone in her voice that implied, "The Bible is not just a book. It's special." And it was . . . it *is*.

For as long as I can remember the Word of God has been the place for me to go for answers and direction— my fundamental guide in making decisions. It was where my family went when others brought us the broken pieces of their lives to be mended and healed. When parents came to the parsonage brokenhearted over a rebellious son or daughter, Daddy would open the Bible and read from the fifteenth chapter of Luke the story of the Prodigal—the wayward son who one day felt his father's love reaching all the way to the pigpen he had made of his life. "There's hope. Keep on loving," Daddy would say. When couples came to plan their future weddings, Daddy would sit with them at our kitchen table and open the Bible. "Husbands, love your wives, even as Christ also loved the church, and gave himself for it," he would read from Ephesians (5:25). Then he'd turn to the hopeful groom. "Are you ready for that kind of commitment . . . forever?" he'd ask.

When I faced hard times at school because of my Christian commitment, Mother and I would read 1 Peter and 2 Timothy. I can remember her saying, "Be sure the hard times are truly because of your Christian choices and not because you lack kindness or good judgment. But if you do the best you can to be kind to everyone and to live at peace 'as much as lieth in you,' then be glad. Many great people have stood in your shoes. It's an honor to be one of them."

Now as an adult I find the Bible is truly the "operations manual" for the construction and maintenance of my life. In our home, in our marriage, in our professional life, in our businesses, Bill and I are constantly faced with increasingly difficult choices. We find that the Bible speaks again and again to give us direction and help.

The need for that kind of direction is especially acute in the mixed-up world we live in today. Our own resources are often simply not enough to make sense out of the confusion that confronts us. In an article in *Psychology Today*, Dr. James Hassett once stated, "Ethical choices cannot be left entirely up to well-bred instincts, good intentions, and broad principles."[1] Instincts can be faulty, good intentions lack power, and the day is passed when we can find in the society around us any clear-cut principles that are ethically dependable. Instead, we live in a world that seems to be endorsing a crazy reverse morality, calling good bad, and right wrong. We seem to be living in the day that Isaiah described when he said people would "say that what is right is wrong, and what is wrong is right; that black is white and white is black; bitter is sweet and sweet is bitter" (5:20, Living Bible).

In my life I have found the Bible to be the only trustworthy compass from which to chart any accurate course through such a world. It has been for me a teacher, a critic, a censor, an encourager, a defender, and a guide. When the society around me staggers from a lack of direction, the Bible offers direction, hope, and certainty.

I have learned the value of God's Word anew from my children. At fourteen my oldest daughter Suzanne was already faced with choices and decisions that boggled my mind. Each night and morning she would read from the Bible for herself in the quiet of her room. Often, when I went up to tell her good-night, she would share her chosen passage with me. One night she said to me, "Mother, do you know why I read like this every day? It's not so much because these verses apply to a particular problem I'm having. It's just the tone of the scripture. Mom, you don't know how it is at school—the things I hear, the values around me. It's so much a part of my day that it's easy to get used to it all, to think it's normal. So I read . . . just to get things back into perspective and to keep it clear in my mind just how God thinks about things."

Of course, she was exactly right—and she had put her finger on an important truth about *how* the Word of God directs us. The Bible can give us specific direction. But—more important—it guides us by helping us know and stay aware of "how God thinks about things." In the craziness of our world then, the Bible becomes our map when we are lost, our light in the darkness. When we come home from our workaday world emotionally or psychologically battered and bruised, it is our balm and encourager. When we feel ourselves becoming acclimated to worldly thinking, the Bible is there to point out our failures and to help us tune back in to eternal values.

When young Timothy was facing comparable situations in his day, Paul reminded him of the wonderful resource he had available to him: "Continue in what you have learned and have become convinced of, because you know those from whom you learned it, and how from infancy you have known the holy Scriptures, which are able to make you wise for salvation through faith in Christ Jesus. *All Scripture is God-breathed and is useful for teaching, rebuking, correcting and training in righteousness, so that the man of God may be thoroughly equipped for every good work* (2 Tim. 3:14-17, NIV, emphasis added).

That kind of help and guidance is available for our lives, too, through the Bible. But it takes time; the full power of the Scriptures comes from a long and intimate relationship with God's Word, not an occasional brief encounter. The Bible is not a spiritual "rabbit's foot." We can't treat it like a sort of "panic potion" and expect it to have power in our lives. If we wait until we are face to face with a crisis before we dust off the "black book," we aren't too likely to find any relevant answers.

"Searching the scriptures" doesn't mean letting the Bible fall open at random and stabbing an index finger at its pages with our eyes shut, hoping to find a magic remedy that will fix everything. On the contrary, only a continuing companionship with God's Word will truly equip us to think clearly when we are faced with choices to make. The Bible helps us know God better. If our motive for reading God's Word is to know God more intimately, then the book that at one time may have seemed to be dull and difficult will take on the excitement of a living adventure.

When Bill and I met, I was in college and he was already teaching. I had grown up in Michigan; he in Indiana. I knew little about his home and family, and even less about his childhood, his high school activities, and his college days. As we started dating and became more and more interested in each other, I found myself wanting to know all about him: Why did he think the way he did? What was he like as a child? Whom did he date in high school? College? When did he become interested in music? The more I came to like him, the more questions crowded into my mind. The more I knew about him, the more I wanted to know. I asked his mother if I could see his old high school yearbooks. She and I spent long afternoons poring over annuals and photo albums from Bill's childhood—pictures of family gatherings, birthday parties, pets, and pastimes. I read old term papers he had written and the thesis he had done for his master's degree.

An attic full of old yearbooks and albums may not sound very exciting to you, but to me they were! I was coming to love this crazy guy, and I wanted to know everything I could about him. When I went home for the summer, Bill and I wrote letters. I practically memorized every word he sent! I couldn't wait for the mail to come at 10:45 every morning. On weekends, just the glimpse of a red convertible would make my heart stop.

In the same way, when Jesus really comes to possess our lives, we want to know everything about Him that we can. We want to know what God is like and what He expects of us. We want to learn the mind of God and how we can make our lives more compatible with His plan for us. When we love Jesus, the Bible no longer seems to be a dull and dusty collection of stories from the past. It becomes a living, breathing clue to the personality of the One who has come to be of ultimate importance in our lives.

I love the verse in Paul's second letter to Timothy that says, "The whole Bible is given to us by inspiration from God." (That's from the Living Bible paraphrase of the passage I quoted earlier.) This verse tells me so much about what the Bible is and how it's supposed to work in my life. First, it tells me that the Bible is a message especially for me, written to speak to my unique set of circumstances. When Bill wrote to me during our courtship, he didn't send one of those letters people send at Christmas time—you know, the kind that has been run off on the mimeograph and sent to everyone on the card list, the kind that is filled with answers to questions nobody asked. No, he wrote to *me*, specifically about *our* plans and *our* dreams, our problems, and sometimes our arguments. In the same way, the Bible is God's special Word for me. It speaks in an uncanny way to just what I'm going through. It is the *living* Word.

Another reason I love that verse is that it says the message God sends in the Bible comes "by inspiration." There is caring behind it. There is energy and involvement. This message isn't sent out of duty or obligation. It is sent out of love! I have felt inspiration, and I know the way it consumes me and drives me beyond the limits of my normal capabilities. To know that the

God of the universe cares so much about me that He was inspired—driven, compelled—to get involved in my life is almost more than I can comprehend.

I am also impressed by the word *whole*—"The *whole* Bible is given to us." That means I can't just snap out the parts I like and ignore the rest. I can't avoid those verses that nail me to the wall. I have to deal with it all, including ones such as, "Let us stop just *saying* we love people; let us *really* love them, and *show it* by our *actions*" (1 John 3:18, Living Bible), and the place that says don't be "like children, forever changing our minds about what we believe" (Eph. 4:14, Living Bible), and "Wives, fit in with your husbands' plans" (1 Pet. 3:1, Living Bible). It means, too, that I can't just take verses out of context to prove my point. I must be done with legalism and with using Scripture as a whip. It means that in preparing to be a good decision maker I must know the Scriptures as a "whole," so that I will know more and more about the character and intent of God.

The Bible is full of stories about people who were faced with choices. Some of them, like Paul and Moses, made wise choices and obeyed God. Some of them failed. David allowed lust to rob him of the best God had for him; he chose to betray the trust given him, and he committed adultery and murder. Peter broke his promises and betrayed his Lord. The people in the Bible are like you and me—real, struggling, vulnerable human beings. And in the scope of God's patience and judgment, grace and anger, forgiveness and mercy, we can see what is required of us in the reality of our days.

This brings us to another crucial point about how the Bible works in our decision making. It is not enough to just read the Bible, even if we read it a lot. As Soren Kierkegaard said, "I do not know the truth until it becomes part of me." We must internalize what we read.

DECISION VISION

Bill and I once wrote a little song that goes like this:

I'm happy to hear that you've been "into the
   Word"
And spending time to study and learn
I'm glad for all the hours you have spent on your
   knees
'Stead of wond'rin' which way you should turn.

You tell me meditation is what the world needs,
And I reckon what you're sayin' is true.
I was glad when I heard you're getting into the
   Word
But is the Word getting into you?

Now don't get me wrong: I'm not puttin' you
   down—
I'm glad for every chapter you've read.
But readin' and doin' are two diff'rent things,
And the Word without the Spirit is dead.
Has it made you more loving to your wife and
   your kids,

Patient and kind, through and through?
Have your attitudes changed since you've been
   into the Word?
Is the Word gettin' into *you*?[2]

It is not enough for me to read Jesus' words in the
Bible, if I do not hear Him speaking to me. I can read
Jesus' invitation to follow Him and the excuses made
by those who hear Him—one person said he had to go
bury his father; another said he had to take care of his
family. I can read Jesus' answer to them: "Anyone
who lets himself be distracted from the work I plan
for him is not fit for the Kingdom of God" (Luke 9:62,
Living Bible). But unless my heart hears Jesus speaking
to me about my priorities and the disproportionate

amount of time, energy, and money I spend on things that will not survive this world, things that are not eternal, then I am denying and obstructing the power of the Word to give me direction in my choices.

How can I read about faithless Peter, who took his eyes off Jesus and began to sink into the sea of Galilee, without recognizing the times when I, too, have started trusting in my own abilities, even God-given abilities, and felt myself sinking in the sea of daily confrontation, tugged by the currents of worldly thinking?

I can read of the rich young ruler who had been brought up in the church—a "model" kid, a young man who had done everything right, kept all the commandments. Not only that—he also had "clout" in the religious community. But Jesus zeroed right in on the real issue: the young man didn't like to risk. He liked his security. He wanted to be in control of his own destiny, and his possessions gave him the security he so valued. "Sell it all," Jesus said, "so you can learn to trust in me. Give everything away that is keeping you from risking. Follow me" (see Luke 18:18-23).

In this passage I must hear Jesus speaking directly to my tendency to hold on, to build a safe nest, to protect my turf. I hear Him say, "Blessed are the poor in spirit, [those who have learned that they have to depend on *me*] for theirs is the kingdom of heaven." And I wonder just what it will take before I really make all my choices in line with Jesus' Kingdom mentality.

In the pages of the Scripture, I see God at work in history, and I know He is at work in my life. In the Word I see the living Christ moving through the chaos of my day—caring, loving, lifting, calling, showing me in living flesh what God is like. In the Scripture I see reflected a value system that is not of this world, an ethic that calls me beyond and lifts me above the materialistic values so prevalent around me. In God's

Word I find assurance that the Holy Spirit has been sent to dwell in me, giving me power to actually make my choices consistent with what my heart believes but my humanness would otherwise hinder.

Best of all, the Bible as a whole brings me to a deeper understanding of the character and intent of God. More and more I learn how my choices stack up in the light of the way God would have me think and choose.

When I was a college student, I was away from home for the first time. At times I felt frightened and alone. Ours had been a close family that was open to one another; home was a place I could go for advice and direction. But away at school I often found myself in situations I had never encountered before. Nothing specific, no rules or instructions, no direct advice, no letters from home were available to me to give me concrete answers to the problems I faced. Sometimes, when I found myself in these new situations, I would think, "If my parents were here to talk with me, what advice would they give me?" Although I didn't have a specific word from them on this new problem, I knew them so well—how they thought, what they had taught, how they felt and reasoned—I could fairly accurately know how they would advise me if they had been there.

For me, this is a good analogy of our relationship with God. Ours is a rich heritage. As Christians our roots run deep throughout human history. In spite of sin and evil, the touch of God on our world and on its people is always clear. We see His fingerprints on all of life—even life today in the closing years of the twentieth century. Now, as throughout all of history, knowing God and understanding His Word prepares us for making the kinds of decisions that will enrich our lives and enable us to grow into the kind of wholeness God wants for us. It should be our goal to know God so well, through making His Word a part of the real fabric of our days, that we can sense, even in this new computer age, what the Father is saying to us about the decisions we face. We *can* know. We have His Word.

FOR WORK AND DISCUSSION

Getting to Know God through the Scriptures

1. Find one or two paraphrases in modern English to use with your favorite translations. (I would suggest J. B. Phillips and the Living Bible Paraphrases, used with the New International Version.)

2. Read a passage first in a good children's Bible story-book—especially when reading the Old Testament. Don't be embarrassed. These are written to make God real to children; it only makes good sense that they will make Him more real to us, too! (Try *Egermeier's Bible Story Book*,[3] revised edition, which has questions in the back, and *Bible Stories* by Norman Vincent Peale.[4]) Doing this will let you cover long portions of Scripture so that you can get the "big picture" and sense the drama and excitement of God at work through history.

3. Have a plan. (Not a plan to "get through" the Bible, but a plan to discover what God is saying through the whole of Scripture.) Perhaps it would be helpful to send for one of the following plans:

> SEARCH THE SCRIPTURES
> InterVarsity Press
> Box F
> Downer's Grove, IL 60515
>
> NAVIGATOR'S DAILY WALK
> P. O. Box 6000
> Colorado Springs, CO 80934

DECISION VISION

YOUR GUIDE THROUGH SUPERNATURAL
LIVING THROUGH YOUR DAILY WALK
Campus Crusade for Christ, International
Arrowhead Springs
San Bernardino, CA 92414

4. Think of your time with the Word as an appointment with the most important loved one in your life, a chance to get to know more about Him. Make that appointment at the best time of the day for your mind and energies: first thing in the morning before everyone else is up, during your noon hour, in the evening when everything else is out of your way and you have the privacy you need.

5. Join or start a growth and Bible study group made up of people who are vitally interested in getting to know the living God through the Scriptures. Try to share, honestly and as openly as a child, the exciting things the Holy Spirit is teaching. Listen. Do not let the group degenerate into a social club or gossip society. Help to keep the focus on the Living Christ and what He has to say.

6. Don't let your study become an exercise in legalism. Don't let your mind trick you into getting hung up on minor details or insignificant theological controversies. Don't use Scripture to "prove a point," but open your heart to the Word and welcome its reproof. It will make you wise (2 Timothy 2:23).

God's Word and My Decision

1. Does the Word of God give specific guidance in this matter?

2. As you weigh each alternative, ask yourself: Would this choice be consistent with what the Scripture tells me about the character and intent of God?

3. Ask: If I am convinced this is the right decision, am I carrying out the decision in such a way that my attitudes and actions are consistent with the character and intent of God?

1. James Hassett, "Is It Right? An Inquiry into Everyday Ethics," *Psychology Today*, June 1981, 49.
2. "Into the Word," lyric by Gloria Gaither. ©Copyright 1982 by Gaither Music Company.
3. Elsie Egermeier, *Egermeier's Bible Story Book*, rev. ed. (Anderson, Ind: Warner Press, Inc.)
4. Norman Vincent Peale, *Bible Stories* (New York: Franklin Watts, 1973).

4

Prayer—Using God's Resources

I pray that Christ will be more and more at home in your hearts, living within you as you trust in him. May your roots go down deep into the soil of God's marvelous love; and may you be able to feel and understand, as all God's children should, how long, how wide, how deep, and how high his love really is; and to experience this love for yourselves, though it is so great that you will never see the end of it or fully know or understand it. And so at last you will be filled up with God himself. —Ephesians 3:17-19, Living Bible

It was a sunny day in late July, and the woods were a fairyland to me as I skipped ahead of Grandma down the well-worn path toward the blackberry patch. Off to one side of the path was what was left of an old blue car someone had deserted years before. I stopped to peek inside, hoping to see whether the family of skunks that had used it for a home in the early spring were all grown by now and moved away. A jay flew low overhead, scolding me for invading her territory. As I got in sight of the big juicy blackberries, I looked back over my shoulder to see if Grandma was catching up, because she had the berry basket. I'll never forget what I saw. There was Grandma kneeling in prayer at an old stump.

It wasn't the only time I'd seen her on her knees. Prayer was as much a part of her life as the bread she baked and the garden she kept. Although I didn't realize it at the time, I understand now the enormity of the decisions she had to face back then, and the problems that could have defeated her.

First of all, Grandma was legally blind, although she had minimal vision with the aid of thick glasses and a hand-held magnifying glass. (This is the way she daily managed to read her well-worn large-print Bible.) The problem and worry caused by the news that her younger son had been wounded while serving in the army and was hospitalized in New Guinea was intensified when a separation from his wife left their baby for Grandma and Grandpa to care for. Grandpa's minimal Social Security payment and Grandma's small pension for the blind were barely enough to make ends meet. Their aging farmhouse had no electricity or indoor plumbing; it was heated by a kerosene space heater.

By almost any standards, Grandma had reason to be discouraged and pessimistic. Yet she fairly sparkled with optimism and seemed to have more time to listen, more food to share, more room to take in someone who was in need, and less tension and stress than anyone else around. I might think that as a child I just didn't notice her distress, but I was not the only person who found comfort in her kitchen or a welcome in her words.

I don't know how she managed to take everything in stride, but I do know this: she took everything to God in prayer. No day began or ended without it. After her death, I found a well-worn piece of paper in her tattered Bible. Written on it in her own shaky hand was this poem:

I met God in the morning
  When my day was at its best,
And His presence came like sunrise,
  Like a glory in my breast. . . .

Then I thought of other mornings,
  With a keen remorse of mind,
When I too had loosed the moorings,
  With the Presence left behind.

So I think I know the secret,
  Learned from many a troubled way:
You must seek Him in the morning
  If you want Him through the day![1]

Grandma was not the only person in my life who taught me the importance and the privilege of prayer. In our home my parents prayed about everything: how we would handle a disgruntled church member, how we would buy the new pair of shoes my sister needed for the basketball team, how we could find room for someone who had no place to live. When people called the house to say there had been an accident, we prayed. When I had a big test at school, we prayed. When Daddy received a call to a new church, we prayed. During the time we girls were dating, our parents prayed a lot!

As I grew up, my life was influenced by several great men and women of prayer. Most of these people were not great theologians or famous churchmen, but they were giants to me because they taught me the way prayer works in a Christian's life. They taught me that prayer wasn't something you *said*; it was the way you *lived*. They showed me the joy of having Jesus for a friend.

There was Minnie Hill, who taught my junior Sunday school class, and who even prayed for her lemon pies to be perfect if they were intended to be a special gift for someone who was hurting. And John Truax, whose speech defect might have kept him from talking clearly enough to witness the way he wanted to if it hadn't been for prayer. His special ministry was hitch-hiking. He thought that being shut in the car with a person going sixty miles per hour down the road was a good chance to have that person's full attention. Whenever a car stopped to pick up Johnny, he would pray that he would be understood, because he was going to be talking about Jesus!

There was Ione, a wonderful part-Indian preacher who pioneered in northern Michigan. Ione just lived every day as though she believed God were on her wavelength. She talked to Him with her mind, con-sciously including the Lord in her daily routine. Often her communion with Him would bring to her mind someone whom she felt had a need or was facing a crisis. She would "lift them up to Jesus." It wasn't uncommon for her to call or drop us a note that said: "God brought you to my mind this week. I don't know what you're going through, but I've been praying for you." Our family looked forward to her occasional visits because we knew they would include precious times of "talking to God" together.

And then there is Sid Guillen, our friend who was born in Cuba. Now an American citizen, Sid is a respected college professor who holds his doctorate in Spanish and is head of the foreign language depart-ment where he teaches. But his greatest credential, as far as Bill and I are concerned, is his simple, childlike belief in prayer. Jesus and Sid know each other, and when Sid prays, you get the feeling that he and Jesus are very used to talking together. The students Sid teaches flock to his office and to his home with the decisions they face—decisions that will determine the directions of their lives. Together Sid, his wife Myrna, and the students take the problems to the Lord. Often the Guillens and the Gaithers have prayed together about major choices we faced. It is wonderful to have friends who can both think and pray.

My sister Evelyn is very special to me as a prayer partner, but I'm not the only person touched by her trust in God and in prayer. Evelyn's ministry is her kitchen and her coffee pot. Through her warm and cozy house files a parade of persons who need to be loved and listened to and prayed with. If you were to show up on her back porch, she would meet you there and flash her big, friendly "welcome in" grin. Soon you'd feel as if you had just "come home," because you'd be sitting at her kitchen table with a cup of hot coffee and a fresh cookie in your hand. Evelyn would sit there with you as though she had all day to do nothing else but be with you, and before you knew it, you would be spilling out all the perplexities you face. Then she would read to you some wonderful verse of scripture she just happened to have read "this very morning," and she'd say, "Well, let's talk to the Lord about it."

From these precious people and many others I have learned a few things about prayer and how vital it is to the Christian's decision-making process. First of all, decisions are hard. Many of the problems we face almost defy human logic. They are gnarled and knotty questions for which our wisdom is just no match. That is why it is such a wonderful privilege to pray! We have, freely offered to us, all the resources of God, who says that we may "come to share in the very being of God" (2 Pet. 1:4, NEB).

How ridiculous to think that we would even try to muddle through the tough decisions of our lives and refuse to take advantage of such an offer! Prayer is sort of like an unlocked door with a giant, red-lettered sign on it that says, "Welcome. Feel Free to Take Whatever You Need." Inside is the storehouse of all that God is. He invites us to share it all. He doesn't intend for us to stay on the outside and struggle all alone with the perplexities of life, and He not only invites us to come in but to stay in, in order that His "Grace and peace be *yours in fullest measure,* through the knowledge of God and Jesus our Lord" (2 Pet. 1:2, NEB, emphasis added).

That leads me to the next thing I'm learning about prayer: It is an ongoing process, not just an occasional religious-sounding speech we make to a nebulous divinity "out there somewhere." Prayer is meant to be a part of our lives, like breathing and thinking and talking.

I used to be confused by verses in the Bible that said we should "pray without ceasing" (1 Thess. 5:17). I thought, Nobody, but nobody, can pray all the time! I couldn't even pray for fifteen minutes straight without my mind wandering. I'd try! I'd set the alarm clock in front of me and determine to pray longer and longer each day. It was useless. Not only could I not do it; I was bored and disillusioned with the attempt. But what did all those references mean—"Seek his face continually" (1 Chron. 16:11), and "praying always with all prayer and supplication in the Spirit" (Eph. 6:18).

Gradually, I have begun to learn that prayer is more like a Jesus-and-me way of living. Brother Lawrence has called this "practicing the presence of God." And that is exactly how the people of prayer I have known live. Prayer is second nature to them. It's not what they do as a last resort. It's not what they do on special occasions. It is, instead, the way they think. They live their lives always knowing that God is there and His resources are always available.

So often, instead of letting prayer do the work for us, we add prayer to our workload and drag it around like the rest of our burden. It becomes one more task we have to face on top of all the never-ending demands on our time and energy.

I remember once going with Suzanne's class to the

Indianapolis 500 Racetrack Museum. In it was a collection of some of the earliest cars. I was intrigued that, although those first cars had headlights, they also still carried lanterns on the sides, just as the old carriages had done. They must not have given much light compared to the new, efficient "electric" beams, but there they were, just the same—just excess baggage. When I was new at prayer, I was sort of like the "horseless carriage." I didn't really trust the new power and privilege I had, and I hung on to my frustrating old habits when I could have used the new light and power.

Prayer is intimate and loving communion between a human person and a holy God. It is the privilege given us by God, then extended to its fullest by the death and sacrifice of Jesus. When Jesus died for us, He tore away all the ceremonial trappings that kept us at arm's length from God, separated from Him by our sin. Because of Jesus we can go directly to God without fear and call Him "Abba, Father" (see Gal. 4:6). That really means "Daddy" to me, for "Abba" was the affectionate personal word children used for addressing their fathers. There's no distance there, no religiosity, just a comfortable, natural relationship. God invites us, because of Jesus, to just be at home in his presence, to call Him "Daddy" and openly tell Him what we need.

I love the verse that says, "Don't worry about anything; instead, pray about everything; tell God your needs and don't forget to thank him for his answers" (Phil. 4:6, Living Bible). Now, that last part is important, too, especially for us. It helps us avoid the "taker" mentality. It's sort of like teaching children to say "thank you." Oh, partly it's for the sake of the person who gives them gifts. But mostly it's for *them*. We want them to understand what it takes to build relationships, to understand other people's sacrifice and love. We want them to grow up being aware that they are debtors and that real love always feels grateful. And we know that greed destroys relationships, but gratitude builds them.

The same principle works in our relationship to God. He wants to "freely give us all things" (Rom. 8:32), but we need gratitude in our lives so that greed will not destroy our openness to God or our love for Him. Greed doesn't destroy God's love for us; it destroys *our* ability to love.

The next verse in Philippians goes on to say: "If you do this you will experience God's peace, which is far more wonderful than the human mind can understand. His peace will keep your thoughts and your hearts quiet and at rest as you trust in Christ Jesus" (4:7, Living Bible).

As we grapple with the choices we face and the decisions we must make, prayer is our unlimited resource. It is the door to all that God is. Prayer, and not worry, will give us peace in the middle of all the chaos, and praise—the attitude of gratitude—will keep us from shrinking inside and keep us open to all God has for us. Together, prayer and gratitude will put our minds at rest, even as we grapple with hard problems.

The Bible is full of examples of people who faced tough decisions and accomplished great deeds because they had open communication with God: Moses, Abraham, Gideon, and Samuel; Hannah, Elijah, Jehoshaphat, and Ezra. Mary, the mother of Jesus, and Elizabeth, the mother of John the Baptist, were women of prayer, and the first thing they did when Mary arrived at Elizabeth's house with the news of her pregnancy was to pray together and thank God for His blessings, even though great problems and perplexities were facing them both.

The early church met often for prayer; Acts records their praying until the house where they met was actually rocking with the presence of the Lord (see

Acts 4:23-31). Mark's mother kept her home open for prayer, and during one of these prayer meetings (in a prison across town), Peter was awakened by an angel to find that his chains were broken and he was free.

Jesus was our greatest prayer-practicing example, and He told us often that we, too, would need the abiding power of constant prayer (prayer-living) if we were to make the choices God wants us to make. Facing the most important decision of history, Jesus went to Gethsemane to pray. Three times He asked that God show him any alternative to what He faced that would still accomplish the goal of redemption. "If it be possible, let this cup pass from me," He prayed (Matt. 26:3), yet He found in prayer the strength to align His will to the will of the Father, to face the cross, and ultimately to win victory over death itself.

Of all the steps we need to take to make wise choices, prayer is, without doubt, the most vital. But, like our relationship with the scriptures, to be truly effective prayer must be a living, daily part of our lives. Panic praying is a weak substitute for a life of constant communion with the Lord. Prayer is not some sort of hocus-pocus incantation we chant in desperation when we get into trouble. The vehicle of prayer in itself has no magical power, and God is no genie who stays quietly tucked away in a jug until we rub it.

In his book *Healing Life's Sore Spots*, Frank Kostyn writes: "There is power in prayer properly used, but this power is hammered out or born from the iron of reality. Prayer is not a marshmallow coating spread over our daily lives so that we may attract various benefits to ourselves. Prayer is not an easy way out of a difficult situation. . . . Prayer is communication with God, but we cannot manipulate God through means of prayer. It cannot be simply a request for whatever we desire, however worthy this desire appears to us. . . . Prayer is our act of trust that the creator has the power to change things, but it also is an act of humility and submission of our will to his."[2]

Prayer changes things, but it also changes us. It helps us lay down our defensiveness and our preconceived ideas. The very act of prayer is an act of opening ourselves to the will of Another. It is choosing to focus our mental faculties on God. It is deliberate submission.

Prayer is natural communication between us and the most important Person in our lives. Jesus instructed us to pray, and His life demonstrated how to develop a life of simple prayer in daily routine. He began His mornings with prayer and was in prayer at the close of day. He taught us to keep prayer simple; He refused to acknowledge as true prayer the high-sounding, rehearsed, and empty repetitions so common in church circles (see Matt. 6:7 and Matt. 23:14). He taught us to pray like children.

Children, too, have taught me to pray. Open and trusting, they tell God about their day, about their needs, about their joys. They assume Jesus is a part of the family who is "in on" everything that is happening around our house.

One time when our children were small we received word that my sister and her family were coming to visit—some very exciting news to our three-year-old daughter. We were just ready to leave the house when the news came, so afterward we went on out to get into the car, only to realize Suzanne was missing. I went back in to see what was keeping her, and found her in her room talking on her little play phone. "What are you doing?" I asked. "Oh, I was just telling Jesus that Lisa is coming!" she answered.

Another time we all had the flu. We took care of each other the best we could, but it was a very bedraggled-looking family that gathered for prayer that night. Amy, then three years old, ended her prayer like this: ". . . and God, please don't let Jesus get my cold." She had taken very literally our statement that Jesus is always very close to us, and she knew that when people get "very close" they sometimes catch each other's illnesses.

We smile at that, but I have been amazed at the power in Amy's prayers. When she prays for someone, there are results. She believes it. She asks it. She knows that Jesus who loves her will take care of her, and He does. I have often gone to her room and asked her to pray with me about one serious situation or another. Sometimes I can't even tell her what the need is, but together we agree in prayer. How wonderful it is that mature trust is unrelated to chronological age. Amy knows Jesus and believes what He said. That is enough.

Our family was on vacation in a secluded area in Puerto Rico. Our children were young, and my mother had gone along to help with them so that Bill and I could get some rest and work on a project with Ronn and Donna Huff.

One afternoon Bill and I took a walk down the beach while mother watched the children at play in the water. We were coming back to where we'd left them when we saw Amy running in the sand waving her arms. When we got close enough, we could hear her shouting, "Suzanne lost her glasses in the ocean! We were looking for shells when a big wave hit her face and washed her glasses out to sea!"

"How long ago?"

"About fifteen minutes."

My mind immediately thought of the rugged coral reef that ran parallel to the shoreline about a hundred fifty feet out and of the game we'd played all week, throwing little objects into the water to see how quickly the strong current carried them up the beach.

When we reached Suzanne she was standing knee-deep in the water swishing her hands through the foam.

DECISION VISION

"What am I going to do?" she wailed. "I can't see a thing without my glasses! We could never get them replaced way out here in this strange place."

I knew she was right. Almost without thinking I said, "Well, the Lord knows all about how much you need your glasses. We're His children and it's His ocean. We'll just pray."

The words had barely passed my lips when I thought to myself, How dumb can you get! Not only is it impossible that those glasses could escape being dashed to pieces on that coral by the strong undertow, but even if they were in one piece the current has carried them far away by now."

But I'd gone too far to turn back now. There I stood knee-deep in the ocean holding the hands of my twelve-year-old daughter while our other two little children stood watching. All I could do was to pray . . .

"Lord, you know about Suzanne's glasses and how much she needs them. You know we're 'way out here on this island. If it's your will . . ." I was trying to give God plenty of room and let Him off the hook just in case . . .

"Mother!" Suzanne squealed, interrupting my careful prayer. "Something just hit my leg!!"

Suzanne reached down past the seafoam into the water and pulled out her glasses—all in one piece and without a scratch.

That night as our family gathered for worship in our hotel room before bed, Psalm 139 hollowed out an unforgettable place in our family's memory: "Though I ride the morning winds to the farthest oceans, even there your hand will guide me, your strength will support me."

One hears all sorts of possible arguments over when and how God answers prayer. All I know is Jesus said he loves us and wants to "freely give us all things even before we ask." We would believe no less had Suzanne not found her glasses because we have

58

come to know that our God can be trusted to be at work for good in all things if we love him. But time and time again we have found him to be involved in the daily affairs of life. The "insignificant" incident on an island beach affirmed for me again that God is at work in the decisions and perplexities of our lives. I would not want to face the complexities of this modern world without that certainty. I can take to Him little things, like losing my wedding ring in the house or Suzanne's glasses in the Atlantic Ocean, and ask Him to help me find them. I can bring Him big things like the future of our children, a crisis in Bill's business, or a new direction in our ministry. Whatever I bring to him, I feel confident knowing that in His storeroom of resources there is always ample supply, even though in my storeroom of resources there is almost never enough. Prayer is not excess baggage in my decision making; it has become my one survival kit.

Now, the decisions I face in my life may seem very insignificant compared to the ones in yours. But no matter how important the choices are, prayer gives us access to all God's resources in making those choices— and that is more than enough!

Wernher von Braun, while director of NASA Space Center, said in an interview:

> Shortly after World War II, I came to understand that religion is not a cathedral inherited from the past, not a quick prayer at the last minute. To be effective, religion has to be backed up by discipline and effort. Gradually, I came to feel that in order to be realistic, my prayers, too, needed to move into a new dimension. I began to pray daily, hourly, instead of on occasion. I took long rides into the desert where I could be alone with my prayer. I prayed with my wife in the evening. As I tried to understand my problems, I tried to find God's will in acting on them. In this

age of space flight and nuclear fission, to use power wisely calls for a moral and ethical climate! We can achieve it only through many hours of deep concentration we call prayer.[3]

FOR WORK AND DISCUSSION

On Prayer

1. Get used to just talking to God. You wouldn't expect to maintain or develop any other relationship (with your spouse, your children, friends) without talking and really communicating, would you?

2. Talk to God as you would any other important person. Don't make speeches to Him; just talk and listen. As with your sister or your wife or child, there are times you will need to make it a point to "have a talk." Other times you will just enjoy being together and let the conversation come naturally. If you were with someone you love and care about, you would never forget that person is there. You would be conscious of their presence and share whatever happens, even in silence. Treat God with the same awareness. He is there. Now. Always.

3. Be eager to learn all you can about God so that you can improve your relationship and your communication. Just as couples like to read old love letters or enjoy going away on marriage enrichment weekends, do all you can to learn more about God. Be curious about Him. Talk to Him about everything.

Prayer and My Decision

1. Have I been really honest with God about this decision? (I may as well. He knows what I'm thinking anyway.)

2. Do I really want to hear what God has to say about this decision?

3. Have I put this decision in His hands? Do I trust His timing or am I rushing in with my own solutions, pushing and shoving to "make it happen."

4. Am I willing to wait without wasting precious energy on worry?

5. Am I saying I'm "waiting on God" when I am really avoiding doing some things I know I have to do? Am I saying I'm being "patient" when I am really procrastinating?

1. Ralph Spaulding Cushman, "The Secret," in *Treasury of Religious Verse*, compiled by Donald T. Kauffman, (Old Tappan, NJ: Fleming H. Revell, 1962), 21.
2. Frank A. Kostyn, *Healing Life's Sore Spots* (New York: Hawthorn Books, 1976), 146-148.
3. Wernher von Braun, Quoted in Kostyn, *Healing Life's Sore Spots*, 149-50.

5

Exactly What Is
the Problem?

Upstairs I could hear the children arguing about something. Their voices got louder and more angry.

"I didn't either!"

"You did too!"

"But I was in here first!"

"You were not!"

"That's my comb anyway!"

"But you took mine to school yesterday and lost it!"

"Well, that's 'cause I was late and had to grab the
first one I saw!"

"That's your problem!"

"No. It's your problem! If you had fed the dogs, I
wouldn't have been late!"

Possibly your house doesn't sound like that in the
mornings before school, but ours sometimes did. Soon
I would have to get involved, and I knew what I'd be
saying; I had said it a thousand times. "Hey! Hold it!
What's the problem here?" Most mornings I ended up
feeling more like Henry Kissinger or Alexander Haig

than like a mother. And I knew I wouldn't get just one clear answer to my question, for there were always many problems.

That day, for instance, by the time three children gave me their view of what the problem was, I had a list that would fill a whole sheet of paper.

—There are too many people in the bathroom.
—There's too little time to get ready.
—Amy's hogging the sink.
—Benjy shoved me!
—Suzanne lost my comb!
—Benjy didn't feed the dogs, so I had to feed them and was late!
—Amy always gets up late!
—Benjy put water on the hairbrush!
—I ruined my hair and I just curled it!
—Suzanne's got on my blue socks, so I had to change to brown cords!
—My socks were dirty!
—We're out of laundry soap!

On and on it went. And when I got to the end of the list, we still hadn't identified the *real* problem.

Our lives as adults are not so different. In the perplexing situations of our lives, the real problem often is . . . *identifying* the real problem. Yet it is impossible to solve a problem or make a decision until we know just what it is we are dealing with.

Did you ever have an argument with your husband or wife over some simple thing, something so silly you couldn't believe that the two of you, grown adults, were standing there hassling over something so stupid? Or did you ever come home from work and find yourself punishing your child for some insignificant infraction that deep inside you realize you might have overlooked or even smiled at on another day? Have you ever found yourself angrily typing your resignation over some incident that had happened a dozen times before?

Such irrational actions are caused by our tendency

to act before we have actually identified the problem. When we don't take the time to focus on the central issue in a given situation, real damage can result. Often decisions made at such highly emotional times may not be recalled. So when and how do we begin to single out the real issue?

The first thing to do when defining the problem is to recognize what the problem is *not*. If I am having an argument with Bill, I have a tendency to bring up everything I haven't had a chance to fuss with him about in the last month. Let's say, for instance, that I have an appointment and am waiting for him to bring me the car. He arrives home later than he promised and forgets to bring from the office some necessary papers that I need to take with me. I manage to keep my cool until I get into the car and discover that the gas gauge is on empty. I am furious! All the time I am getting gas, all the time it takes to go to the office for the needed papers, all the while I am speeding to my appointment, the pressure is building. In my mind I begin to list all the thoughtless things he has done in the whole last week. All through the appointment my anger is simmering on the back burner of my mind. I keep thinking of all the times I just kept my mouth shut and went on. Not only that, I think, I have run errands for him, cancelled plans for him, entertained his friends. . . . So, by the time I get back home, I am seething inside.

Then Bill says something. Perhaps it's a simple question like, "What's the matter, honey?" Or maybe he offhandedly says, "Is tomorrow night all right for us to have the couples in the office over for dinner?" Whatever he says, what happens next has very little to do with my willingness to cook dinner for some associates. Whatever we eventually identify as the problem, *the dinner isn't it!*

Obviously, until we both come to grips with our ultimate goals and identify the obstacles that stand in our way, we can never begin working together to make the changes we need to make to reestablish a clear and loving relationship. Knowing and discussing what the real problem is *not* sometimes helps us to focus on the deeper issues that surface in little ways.

The second step in defining a problem is to recognize the issues that are only peripheral, the things that might be vaguely related but are not the central issue. If, for instance, you as an employer are considering someone for a job, it is necessary to consider those things that effect that person's performance in that particular job. Let's say a person is needed who can work well with the public, can type sixty words per minute, and has a good command of the language. The job will demand that the person have integrity and be able to keep certain information confidential. Other qualities the applicants have may not relate to your specific problem—the problem of finding the best employee available for that position. Whether the applicant is tall or short, slim or heavy, married or single, black or caucasian, just out of college or middle-aged should not be related to this decision. If on the other hand, you were choosing a marriage partner, any of those things might prove to be important as you make your choice.

The third step in focusing on the problem itself is to try to eliminate the emotional overtones that shade and color our sense of reason. It is imperative to zero in on the real problem, not on how we feel about it or on how we have been hurt or helped in the past by those involved in the problem. It is important that we try to empty our decision-making of any excess emotional baggage ahead of time, so that we can see the problem clearly, uncolored by a prejudiced viewpoint.

Perhaps this can best be explained by saying that there are certain times that are not good for making decisions. When I buy groceries for my family I have found it a mistake to shop for groceries just before lunch. That is definitely *not* the time to be making choices about what we need to eat. Grocery stores seem to be arranged in a special way to booby-trap me when I'm hungry. Right out there in front are the potato chips and the fancy desserts, the irresistible breads. No, I do the most sensible grocery shopping *after* lunch when I can think clearly about calories and economical cuts of meats.

It is best not to make decisions during times of great emotional upheaval—right after the death of a loved one, during a painful divorce, on the rebound from a broken romance, or while experiencing heartbreaking situations with children. Depression, too, can destroy our ability to define and identify problems.

I have also found that it is not a good idea to define problems or make decisions when I am angry, for anger certainly hinders clear thinking. Even at those times when anger is a positive emotion (anger over injustice, world hunger, governmental or ecclesiastical waste), it is best used to alert us to the issues. Finding effective and creative solutions requires devotion, hard work, and logical planning, and all these qualities are difficult to come by when we are angry.

The old saying, "Count to ten before you fire" has some validity. It is easy for us to approach problems by reacting rather than rationally acting when our emotions are allowed to motivate us and cloud our vision. Sometimes actually doing something physical helps us to get a better perspective. Running around the block, swimming ten laps in the pool, or doing some calisthenics may help us look at a decision more clearly. Some people find actually writing their feelings on paper helpful—including all the reasons for their anger. Our faulty logic tends to be more recognizable when we see it written in black and white.

I knew a family once who had been plagued with marriage and relational problems. After they committed their lives to Christ, they felt that for them moving to a different house was necessary. There were so many horrible memories lurking in every corner that they wanted a new place to begin their fresh start. Their new house was simple, but it gave them a chance to begin the real work of restructuring their lives without the haunting memories their old house held for them. Changing houses may be a bit drastic for most of us. But it might be helpful to find new surroundings just for a few minutes or hours, to get away from an emotionally charged setting. We might take a walk in the woods or the park, spend a night in a motel or with some loving friends, drive down a road we've never taken before—whatever it takes to steady us emotionally before tackling a problem.

Good decision making is not a mindless emotional reaction. It is a Spirit-controlled, clear-thinking process, part of our pilgrimage to wholeness. Whether our choices are major or relatively insignificant, it is impossible to make them if we don't know exactly what they are. In those cases where the problems are complex and interrelated, it will be necessary for us to work at sorting them out according to their urgency and importance. Then with our goals in view and our obstacles defined—and with a firm foundation of prayer and Bible study—we can set about the task of finding the best possible solutions.

There is a poem by Sara Teasdale in which she describes her pilgrimage as a climb up a mountain. Her motivation for climbing to the top is to stand for one glorious moment at the summit and drink in the view. But because she keeps being distracted by the brambles along the path that keep catching at her skirt, she passes the summit without noticing and has started down the other side before she realizes what has happened. She writes:

I must have passed the crest awhile ago
    And now I am going down—

Exactly What Is the Problem?

Strange to have crossed the crest and not to know,
But the brambles were always catching
the hem of my gown.*

In our lives it's not so much the effort of making decisions that troubles us; it is the effort we spend on small distractions along the way. Sometimes they so drain our energies that we have little left to devote to the real "climb" and may even miss our goals because of a lack of true focus. In defining the real task and in ridding ourselves of distractions, we have the help of the Holy Spirit whose presence illuminates and empowers. Remember, He wants you to make it to the top of your mountain and stand at last triumphant at the top!

FOR WORK AND DISCUSSION

1. Think of the situation you face. Make a list of everything that you perceive to be problems in this situation. Check off all the ones you feel certain are not the real problem.

2. Of the items that remain on your list, rate the "problems" or "obstacles" in order of importance. What is the deepest, primary problem? What aspect of this situation is most urgent? (These must be dealt with first.)

3. Ask yourself: Is my view of this situation being colored by any of these:
   —my anger?
   —my love or deep emotional involvement?
   —my prejudices?
   —my own emotional needs?
   —my grief or sadness?
   —my hurt?
   —my loneliness?

---

*Reprinted with permission of Macmillan Publishing Co., Inc. from "The Long Hill" in *Collected Poems* by Sara Teasdale. © Copyright 1920 by Macmillan Publishing Co., Inc., renewed 1948 by Mamie T. Wheless.

6

Finding and Facing the Facts

Yes, if you want better insight and discernment, and are searching for them as you would for lost money or hidden treasure, then wisdom will be given you, and knowledge of God himself. —*Proverbs 2:3-4, Living Bible*

Having prepared ourselves for facing a decision by defining our goals and objectives, becoming intimate with God's Word, and maintaining a vital personal relationship with God through prayer—and having taken steps to isolate and recognize the specific problem we are dealing with in a particular situation—we are ready to begin the actual process of decision making.

The process has three vital parts:

1. We must collect all the possible data and information available to us that pertains to the problem.
2. We must omit nothing and try to be as unprejudiced as possible in weighing each factor.
3. We must consider each alternative solution and think it through to its logical conclusion.

It is impossible to make a wise evaluation of a

situation given only part of the facts. One day our little nephew was watching The Bill Gaither Trio on a Billy Graham Crusade television special. He was excited to see someone in the family actually singing on the screen!

"Boy, Mom," he said to his mother, "Uncle Bill is really doing a good job, isn't he?"

"Pretty good," his mother answered.

"Did you hear them say that there are sixty thousand people there? He's really drawing big crowds these days!"

"Yes," answered his mother, "And Billy Graham isn't doing so badly, either."

Sometimes for one reason or another we rush into making judgments based on surface information. I talked to a friend the other day who had the unpleasant task of firing one of the secretaries in his office. When she was hired, she had presented a very impressive résumé and statement of her qualifications, and she had been hired on the basis of that statement without any on-the-job demonstration of skills. At first, since she was new at the job, she had been given simple clerical tasks. Then, as time went on, more difficult jobs had been assigned to her. But she had proved unable to do any of them adequately without constant advice and supervision. Whoever hired her had not gotten all the facts; the result was months of inconvenience for the people in the office—not to mention disappointment for the secretary and the unpleasantness of dismissing her for the boss.

Sometimes our prejudices encourage us to overlook certain facts. We "stack the cards" in favor of a predisposed verdict. Often we do this to protect ourselves or to favor someone we love. It is difficult, for example, to be objective about the abilities and qualifications of a person we might not like very much. On the other hand, it is easy to overlook the shortcomings and deficiencies of someone who is pleasant and charming. There are times when our "want to's" get in the way of our "shoulds."

One day when our daughter was in elementary school she came home in tears. She said she'd had an awful day at school because the teacher had been unfair and had given an unannounced test over some material she hadn't even read. She said the teacher had announced that anyone who didn't pass this test could not expect to get an *A*, no matter what kind of work they'd done on other tests. Knowing our daughter to be usually a truthful child and a conscientious student, I decided to visit the teacher and express my objection to such tactics.

When I discussed the matter with the teacher, I learned that Suzanne had not lied to me . . . exactly. She had, however, failed to tell me that (1) she had been out of the room on a special-privilege pass when the assignment had been given; (2) she had failed to get the missed assignment, though she had been told this was her responsibility whenever a pass was given; (3) the teacher had warned the students several times in the preceding week that because of their talking out of turn in the classroom (of which Suzanne had been a part) there would be an unannounced quiz in the following week on which grades would be taken; and (4) because the classroom behavior had slowed the progress so much that only four tests had been given in the grading period, this test would count heavily in the total grade. Much to my embarrassment, I had made the decision to criticize the teacher's action based on only part of the facts and on a predisposition toward a little girl I loved very much.

Of course, children are not the only offenders when it comes to telling only part of the truth. There have been times when I have been guilty of reporting only the facts that made me look good or kept me from seeming to be foolish. There was the time I kept my mouth shut, hoping Bill would not notice that the molding on the garage door had been replaced and freshly painted, and the time I did say that the new dress I'd bought *was* on sale for half price, but did not mention that I had bought *two*.

To make wise decisions, then, we must learn to collect all the facts, even those we would rather ignore. Having done this, the next step is to do our best to weigh each one fairly and objectively. But, as we saw in the previous chapter, being objective about our problems and decisions is often difficult.

Situations that relate to close personal relationships are probably the hardest to make objectively and carefully. It is easy for someone who is not involved to stand around and tell us, "Don't get emotional." It's simple for me to say what I'd do if I were you, or for you to glibly recite easy answers to me. It's even simple sometimes to tell ourselves rationally what we *should* do and feel, but the actual doing and feeling don't come so easily.

One time we had the difficult task of letting an employee go, not because he was doing his job poorly, but simply because there was no real job in our organization for which he was suited. It had become obvious that this person would never go on to develop his own potential as long as he had the security of a position in an established organization. He was basically doing odd jobs when he should have been working at becoming something special on his own. We had come to care a great deal for this young man, so it was not easy to let him go or to say good-bye. On the surface, the decision we had to make seemed to be merely a professional one. But love and caring made it much more.

We all have to face decisions that are difficult to make because we are close to the people those decisions involve. Parents may have to say no to their children when it's time for the children to take responsibility on their own. A wife may face telling her husband that she feels the need to work outside the home—not for the income the job will produce, but for the chance to really make a difference or to revive a lost sense of value. Or a husband may consider a midlife career change because he has come to feel like a human money machine, trapped in a meaningless job by the need to make payments on a house that's too big and buy gadgets nobody really needs.

Decisions like these *are* hard, because they involve us so personally. But, for that same reason, they are especially important. Relationships might make decisions difficult, but they also make them worthwhile! Between husbands and wives, parents and children, neighbors and friends, employers and employees, there must be a caring that goes beyond the surface pleasantries that maintain the status quo.

One of the reasons decisions involving personal relationships are so difficult is that they require deep communication—and a great deal of effort is required to keep peeling away the protective layers our egos insist on building around our hearts. There may be times when situations have been allowed to go on and on without honest communication for so long that the process of peeling away the defenses can be very difficult. The only thing that gives us the courage to tackle such a formidable task is love—a deep sense of caring that goes beyond the pain of the process straight to the awareness that there is a real person down there somewhere who is worth reaching out to.

Sometimes it is just hurried life-styles and hectic schedules that keep us from dealing with the real people and issues in our lives. At times Bill and I have been just too busy to resolve personal problems and make right decisions. I can remember times in our marriage when we just couldn't find time for an argument. We couldn't discuss a problem because there just wasn't a good time to bring it up. We didn't want to waste the limited time we had with the children to go off alone and discuss it, knowing that once the subject was introduced it might "take a while."

We couldn't discuss our problems on the road in planes or buses. We didn't want to bring them up in the dressing room just before a concert; I always get teary and neither of us is good at hiding feelings. Besides, the audience deserved our best energies. Then we weren't able to discuss them on Monday morning because there were "big" decisions that needed all of Bill's attention at the office. So we'd let them slide. Usually, the pressure would build and build until some stupid, insignificant happening would make one of us explode. So much for assimilating all the facts and data! So much for being as unprejudiced as possible in weighing each factor! So much for considering every alternative and thinking it through to its logical conclusion! Out would pour all the garbage we'd been collecting to tell each other for weeks.

Because we had failed to deal honestly with the small problems as they came up, a major confrontation would result. With emotions high and the real issue clouded with unresolved peripheral problems, the task of thinking objectively and making good choices becomes very difficult. Unnecessary hurt may be the result.

I don't believe that the answer is for Christian couples never to have disagreements and confrontation. On the contrary, Bill and I have found that our marriage is healthier when we can find time for honest confrontation *more often*. That way we can manage to deal with issues one at a time, no matter how small they are, and to resolve them before they become blown out of proportion.

Actually, I believe the real culprit for our failure to do this is probably the time pressure we live with. We all live at a breakneck pace these days. Time and circumstances push us all into a pressure-cooker process of decision making and keep us from approaching decisions with the Word, prayer, and a clear head. If our relationships are strong and deeply rooted in a forever commitment, they probably will survive the pressures of time and the eruptions that result from putting off problems too long. But eventually we have to come to grips with the fact that often our pace is hectic because we have made some unwise choices about budgeting our time. Something has gone awry in our priorities, and we must take steps to protect and nourish those relationships most important in our lives.

Keeping priorities straight in a world that seems to pull at us from all sides is not easy. Brainwashed by the media to believe that we should be some kind of superperson, we take on much more than one person can realistically accomplish and then wonder why we spend our days on the frantic edge of hysteria. The materialistic world around us pushes and squeezes to get us into its mold of spending a high percentage of our energies to generate more and more income. The social world pressures us to feel guilty if we don't join a dozen charitable community organizations.

The church has become so institutionalized that instead of encouraging us to simplify our lives and homes and bear each others' burdens, it instead adds to our guilt trip if we don't segment our family and "take an active part" in the "life of the church." That, all too often, means joining youth groups that play and have pizza parties, men's fellowships that watch films of old ball games, and women's groups that use "prayer request time" as an excuse for the latest gossip. School activities pull at us. Television robs us of our time to talk and play together; even family disagreements that offer a chance for values and opinions to be expressed are sedated into silence by television. Most of us find ourselves frustrated, doing a lot of jobs we don't really want to do at the expense of time to do what we really want—and at the expense of time to do what we need to do to maintain and nourish our precious relationships with God, our families, and those whose lives could be changed by a profound one-to-one encounter.

We often hear people say, "It's the quality of time that matters, not the quantity," That may be true, but it is also true that quality time takes time! It doesn't happen in a hurry. Quality time isn't filling the moments with some currently in-vogue activity. Rather, it is time spent sharing our deepest feelings with each other and really listening to what is said as well as to what isn't said. In the mad rush of today's world we need to allow for time to waste, to settle in, to get comfortable, to let talk happen without pressure. There has to be time to let each person in the relationship see the other as the best, perhaps the *only*, option for sharing and enjoyment—no TV, no parties, no "Top 40," no friends on the telephone, no mechanical diversions. Just each other. That's the best atmosphere for thoughtfully weighing all the facts in those important relational decisions.

Once we have done our best to collect all the data available and to weigh the facts as objectively as possible, we can sort out the facts we have gathered and consider all the possible directions those facts could take us. Sometimes it is helpful to list all the available alternatives on paper, and under each alternative list the positive and negative results that would come from that solution. We might ask, "What will this decision mean a month from now, a year from now, ten years from now?" What will be its effects on others not necessarily directly involved? Will it be hurtful or helpful in the long run?

Those words *the long run* are crucial. Considering long-term goals and values can make all the difference in choosing the best of the possible alternatives.

Lou and Carol were a young Christian couple with four small children. Lou worked for Carol's father in a jewelry store, a job that paid enough to cover the rent on their house, the payments on their second-hand car, and the living expenses for their frugal budget. They had managed to save a few dollars each month for a down payment on a future home of their own. While Lou worked long hours, Carol cared for the children—the youngest barely a year old. Although with careful planning they managed to avoid going deeply into debt, there was little money—or energy— left to afford Carol and Lou any little extras, such as the occasional night out together they felt they needed to keep their marriage aglow. They were a loving family that enjoyed simple, happy times with their children, but Carol and Lou were sensitive enough to know they needed some special moments alone to enjoy each other, too.

About this time, a friend invited them to share a trip to London. Part of their way would be paid if they could come up with the rest of the money for expenses. Carol and Lou discussed the offer. They decided that although at the moment they couldn't really afford the trip, in the long run it was exactly what their life and their marriage needed. So they sold their car, took their savings, and made the two-week trip— just the two of them.

Some of their more practical friends thought they were crazy to "waste" the money just when they were beginning to get ahead. A few criticized their leaving their four children for two weeks. But Carol and Lou had a wonderful time and came home spiritually and emotionally refreshed—more in love than they had ever been. Their children were well cared for by Lou's parents and had experienced their first lesson in taking responsibility in their parents' absence. The whole family was enriched because of the trip, and eventually they were even able to get another car and a house of their own.

Two years later, Carol and the children were enjoying a friend's swimming pool one hot July afternoon. Lou got off work and went to join the family at the pool. The railroad he always passed had no light, only a fading sign, and the summer weeds had grown tall around the track. He didn't even see the train.

In spite of everything the doctors could do, Lou lived only a few hours. When Carol was given the news, she faced the task of telling her four children, the oldest now only eleven. She put her arm around her young son's shoulders—shoulders she prayed would be strong enough to carry the heavy load she was about to hand him. "Daddy didn't make it," she began, "He's gone to be with the Lord. But in spite of everything, we have a lot to be thankful for. You've had a very special dad. He loved you so. One of his great joys was spending time with you. You probably have had more fathering in your eleven years than most kids have in a lifetime."

Then she paused, lost in thoughts of her own. "I'm so glad we went to London. . . ."

Of course Carol and Lou could never have known at the time how important their decision would become. But they were wise enough to think beyond their immediate material goals to consider the goals that would last. They made their decision for the good of their marriage and their home, not just for the good of a house and a car.

Sometimes there are decisions that seem to be simple and obvious at the time but in the long run will be damaging or evasive. At other times, a rather painful decision may turn out to produce the best and kindest outcome for everyone concerned.

Greg had worked at his job for over a year. He suspected that his foreman was not being totally honest with the company. He had even heard him brag about "walking off" with tools or product that belonged to the company. One day his foreman asked Greg to take part in a scheme to falsify some records and make a little profit on the side. Greg knew that he personally could not go along with the plan, and he refused to do so. A bigger problem faced him, however. As a Christian, shouldn't he report the questionable activities to the head of the department? Greg felt sure that if he did, he would lose his job, because lay-offs were already rumored and management was reportedly watching for ways to cut back. He felt sure his department would be shut down if the situation were discovered.

Still not knowing what he would do for a job should he be laid off, Greg decided that as a Christian he had no choice.

Sure enough, the department was closed, and Greg lost his job. He went home the day he got his notice, concerned about his future, yet confident that he had made the right decision. That night around ten o'clock, Greg got a phone call from an uncle he hadn't heard from in months. The uncle said he had some extra money that he felt impressed to invest in Greg, because Greg had always been so dependable and honest. Could he use the money?

Greg couldn't believe his ears! He had had a secret dream of starting a small business; now was his chance. He started his project and, a little at a time, made it succeed. But that wasn't the end of Greg's story. A few years later, the department head for whom Greg had worked in the original company approached Greg about a new venture, and Greg was able to use the knowledge he gained from running his own business to move into management.

Frequently we may find that when a decision is to be made, there are persons around who are glad to offer easy advice. They see "simple" ways for us to "get out of it" or "take the heat off." But serious decision making requires that we think beyond the immediate, because our decisions must go deeper than merely relieving a current pressure. A properly made and thought-out decision will solve problems, not create them.

Short-sighted solutions are often the breeding ground for far-reaching infections in our personal relationships. Putting Band-Aids on a skin cancer may cover an unpleasant sight, but the disease will continue to grow, infecting new, healthy tissue. A long-term cure requires accurate diagnosis and prompt, often painful treatment. By the same token, facing all the facts, no matter how hard it may be to do so, analyzing with courage and objectivity what must be done if a long-range solution is to be effected, and then accepting that solution honestly is, in the final analysis, the most healing way to go in making difficult decisions. The route of honesty and integrity may not always be the easiest, but it pays tremendous dividends in the end.

There are times when the most honest, far-sighted solution to a problem is also a solution that will involve conflict or controversy. In situations like these, I feel a need for courage to engage in Christian confrontation. Some people mentally picture a Christian as a milk-toast type—meek and mild. They feel that if we are "Christian," we'll never rock the boat or upset anybody, that a Christian parent is one who never crosses his or her child, and a good minister is one who never upsets anyone in the congregation. Love is defined as some kind of bland, anything-goes acceptance of each person's "humanness," and life as the stale existence in the "trap of the human condition."

But the life that is exemplified for us by the Jesus of Scripture, aligned with the requirements of a Holy God and infused with power and energy from the Holy Spirit, is anything but bland or ineffectual. The Jesus of the Scripture is a living example of decisive action and courageous confrontation.

Jesus confronted society's disregard for the personhood of children when He said, "Suffer the little children to come unto me, and forbid them not: for of such is the kingdom of God" (Mark 10:14), and "Except ye be converted, and become as little children, ye shall not enter into the kingdom of heaven" (Matt. 18:3).

Jesus challenged prejudice against despised races, against women, and against social outcasts when He chose to announce who He was first to the adulterous Samaritan woman at the well. He chose the hated Zacchaeus to be His dinner host, and defied legalism by healing and forgiving on the Sabbath. He called the tax collector, Matthew, to be one of His own disciples. There was not a single distortion of God's law in the society of His day that Jesus did not confront and challenge. His meekness was a chosen gentleness issuing from a deep certainty of the rightness of His mission and the strength of His purpose.

What we sometimes call meekness in ourselves is, in reality, cowardice. Because of our fear of conflict or rejection, we avoid confrontation and call our avoidance "kindness." We escape problem-solving and mislabel our abdication "love." We weary of the struggle and call our lack of staying-power "patience." But true patience perseveres; true kindness thinks ahead to the end result. True love risks itself—risks not being loved—for the ultimate good of the loved one. Authentic strength is meek, for it has nothing to prove, and real meekness is strong, for it is convinced that it is pure and has no ulterior motives.

To get tired of facing and dealing with problems is human. Sometimes we just wish they'd go away. When people don't respond or when we have to wait a long time to see the result of a decision, we would like to just give up the struggle. As a parent, I sometimes get tired of disciplining my children. There are days it doesn't seem worth the hassle. I'd like to just turn my head this one time and not notice that homework isn't done, music lessons aren't practiced, manners are shabby, words are unkind, actions are selfish.

DECISION VISION

Perhaps you work in a situation that does nothing to encourage or reward integrity. There may be days when you feel like "What's the use? Why keep being so conscientious? Nobody else around here is breaking his neck to get things done, and besides, who will notice anyway?" In tough work situations it has been helpful for me to remind myself that my real employer is the Lord. When I get discouraged I like to read Ephesians 6:6: "Don't work hard only when your master [boss] is watching . . . work hard and with gladness all the time, as though working for Christ" (Living Bible).

Why keep choosing to do right? Because it *is* right, and because we have thought our choice of doing right clear through to its final result. Paul says in Galatians 6:9; "Let us not get tired of doing what is right, for after a while we will reap a harvest of blessing if we don't get discouraged and give up" (Living Bible).

There are times when to avoid confrontation, to take the easy way out, to just be "nice" and not rock the boat may be easier now, but might be "criminal kindness" in the long run. Letting children think an unacceptable behavior is acceptable does nothing to give them the kind of character and integrity they will one day need. To remain silent about a shady deal may avoid a hassle, but we have to live with ourselves afterward—and the company for which we work has to live with our decisions. The easier way for a pastor might be to resign rather than to deal with immorality in high places. But if he responds this way, what kind of legacy is he or she leaving for the children in that church? What kind of statement is being made to those who trust him or her and will judge the church by that decision?

It was a Michigan springtime morning. I bounded out the back door of our house and ran across the yard to the hedge. The cool dew still sparkled on the grass, but the warm sun promised a play-outside day. I sprawled on the ground as near as I could get to the sweet-smelling lilac bush, and lay on my back looking into the wonderfully blue sky. Spring holds an excitement for a seven-year-old girl, and it almost took my breath away. I loved life! I loved the earth. "I love me, too!" I thought, as I flung my arms around myself.

Then I saw it. On the underside of a lilac leaf was a huge cocoon. It was polished with dew, and the sun shining on it made the silky threads look like satin. As I watched, the funny cocoon gave a sudden jerk. Something was alive inside! Some kind of creature was trapped in there that wanted out!

I noticed a tiny hole in one end of the cocoon, and I could see the little insect move around until it was tired, rest, then struggle again. I will help him, I thought. I pulled the cocoon from the tree and, bit by bit, I tore the tough, silky threads back to open the cage. The warm sun and the cool breeze struck the wet little creature. But to my surprise he did not stretch his wings and fly away; instead he only gave a feeble shudder and lay dead in my hand.

That was not the last time I have had to learn that short-sighted solutions bring sometimes tragic results. "Fixing" a situation isn't always the answer. Simply removing obstacles for ourselves or for those we love might not actually be the most loving thing to do.

It is hard to watch our children struggle through painful situations, and it isn't easy to face a problem we could avoid. It is painful to make a decision others won't understand and we may not be at liberty to defend. But when we carefully consider the end results of our alternative choices, we know we really have to choose rightly. It's the only path to inner peace and hope.

DECISION VISION

FOR WORK AND DISCUSSION

As you face your specific decision, ask yourself:

1. Do I have all the facts concerning this problem? Have I honestly tried to uncover all the information I can find? Are my sources reliable?

2. Have I let my prejudices obscure some facts or weigh some of them more heavily than I should? Have I really been objective in my evaluation of both the problem and the personalities involved?

3. What are all the possible solutions? What would be the final result of each alternative? Would any secondary repercussions result from this decision? Are all these alternatives morally right as far as I can determine from my knowledge of Scripture and from prayer? What would Jesus do? How would He go about it?

7

Seeking Wise Counsel

To learn, you must want to be taught. To refuse reproof is stupid. —*Proverbs 12:1, Living Bible*

I think it was Mark Twain, Grandma Moses, or someone equally perceptive who said, "Learn from the mistakes of others: you can't live long enough to make all the mistakes yourself." Anyway, that statement is one of the lessons life works hard at teaching us all.

No matter how efficient, smart, or independent we happen to think ourselves to be, sooner or later we run into a brick wall that our intelligence or experience cannot handle for us. We can fake it, avoid it, or blunder through it. But a better solution would be to find someone who has walked that way before and has gained wisdom from the experience.

I guess the more immature we are, the more of life's lessons we have to learn from our own experience. When our first baby was a toddler, I spent much time and many words telling her that the stove that heated our old farm house was hot. She could even say the word *hot* back to me. But she still insisted on trying to touch the stove. One day she ventured near the stove and my grandfather said, "Stick your finger against it and see if it's hot." She did. It was. Now she knew from experience, and she never touched the stove again.

As we grow, however, we learn that we can avoid a lot of mistakes and pain by learning from the experiences of others. One of the first signs of maturity seems to be the ability to recognize and admit what we *don't* know and then listen to someone who does.

Our family has an excellent family doctor. Dr. Shafer has come to be a dear family friend, as well as a physician we deeply trust. If you were to ask why we trust him so much, we would have to say it is not for his great medical knowledge, though he is medically knowledgeable and current. It is not his membership in impressive medical organizations, though he has had his share of prestigious appointments. It is not because of his fame in some specialized field, for he has chosen to spend his life as a general practitioner in our small Indiana farming community.

The reason we value our doctor so highly is that he is a kind and caring person who has the rare wisdom of knowing when to say, "I don't know, but I know someone who will." We have decided as a family that a doctor who combines adequate knowledge, personal integrity, and an accurate evaluation of his own abilities is a wise man indeed. It is good to know that, when he speaks, we won't have to make allowances for his insecurities. He is not protecting his ego but is looking out for the well-being of his patients, even when that means referring them to someone else for treatment.

It is a myth that wise persons don't listen to anybody. The fact is, the wiser one becomes, the sooner and more actively he or she seeks counsel. The heavier the burden of responsibility, the greater the need for surrounding ourselves with good, clear-thinking advisers. Perhaps one of the best indicators of an able leader is the quality of the persons to whom he or she listens. World figures have risen or fallen on their capacity for choosing and using wise counsel.

Every four years, on the first Tuesday in November, most of us go down to our precinct polls to vote. When we close the curtain in the voting booth and make our selection for president of the United States, we make our choice not because we're convinced that that person is an expert on world finance, foreign affairs, negotiations, labor relations, interstate commerce, and international law. Instead we pull the lever on the name of the candidate we feel confident can choose the best authorities in all those areas and then use their advice to the best advantage in running the country.

Corporate executives learn very quickly that their success depends on their ability to find persons who are remarkable in certain specialized areas and then encourage them to function at their full capacity. A good manager is not uncomfortable or insecure when surrounded by people who know more than he or she does; it is, in fact, his or her job to locate superior human resources and utilize as much of their potential as possible. Positions of leadership demand the ability to seek out, listen to, evaluate, and appropriate advice.

I once knew a highly trained and capable manager whose credentials and actual abilities were excellent. Yet he failed in his position of leadership because his personal hang-ups and insecurities kept him from listening to the very people he had chosen to advise him. Employees who answered to him were constantly reminded that they were underlings. Creative ideas were belittled when they were suggested, yet often would be introduced later by the executive himself as his own. This man was suspicious of open communication and camaraderie among the staff members, and he demanded that all questions be directed to him alone. Eventually, he lost the confidence and respect of his associates and was moved out of the position of leadership, even though his personal skills were sorely missed.

Utilizing wise counsel is equally important when making decisions on the personal level. Each of us can only see from where we stand; it is impossible for us to perceive an issue clearly except from our own perspective.

John Powell in his book *Fully Human, Fully Alive* states it this way:

> Through the eyes of our minds, you and I look out at reality (ourselves, other people, life, the world and God). However, we see those things differently. Your vision of reality is not mine and, conversely, mine is not yours. Both of our visions are limited and inadequate, but not to the same extent. We have both misinterpreted and distorted reality, but in different ways. We have each seen something of the available truth and beauty to which the other has been blind. The main point is that it is the dimensions and clarity of this vision that determine the dimensions of our worlds and the quality of our lives. . . . If we are to change—to grow—there must first be a change in this basic vision, or perception of reality.[1]

When facing a decision we must have as clear a vision of reality in the matter as possible. And, if we are to be good decision makers, we must actively seek ways to broaden our vision. We must accept the fact that one lone viewpoint can give only partial perception. Evaluating a problem accurately, then, involves gathering as many reliable viewpoints as possible. Then we can begin to decide for ourselves what the true picture is. Reliable counsel will help us approach the problem with openness and will save us from making faulty judgments from our own myopic view.

If the problem is especially close to our hearts, our emotions are likely to color our viewpoint even more. When someone I love is involved or when the problem entails a decision about something I strongly want to do, I find that thinking objectively is difficult. At times like these I find it very helpful to get as many other viewpoints as I can from caring people who can offer me perspective.

Proverbs advises us to "Love wisdom like a sweetheart; make her a beloved member of your family" (Prov. 7:4, Living Bible). Sometimes it is difficult to put aside our own pet view of things and listen to facts we would rather not hear. It is tempting to take the coward's way and listen to cheap advice from acquaintances who will flatter us by agreeing with our opinions. The writer of Proverbs compares such counsel to the smooth words of a prostitute—easy to hear, but tragically costly in the end. He advises us to choose instead the more difficult course of seeking out real truth and courting it like a much adored sweetheart, sparing nothing to win "her," no matter the cost. In the end, then, wisdom will become our faithful companion and will sweeten all the days of our lives.

In my own life, I have often found that knowing I should listen to good advice is one thing; really doing it without becoming defensive is another. But I have learned some steps I can take that help me prepare my heart to receive good advice. Receptiveness is an attitude of the heart, and Paul, in his letter to young Timothy, lists some helpful suggestions for preparing the heart to listen:

Turn your back on the turbulent desires of youth and give your positive attention to goodness, faith, love and peace in company with all those who approach God in sincerity. But have nothing to do with silly and ill-informed controversies which lead inevitably, as you know, to strife. And the Lord's servant must not be a man of strife: he must be kind to all, ready and able to teach: he must have patience and the ability gently to correct those who oppose his message. He must always bear in mind the possibility that God will give them a different outlook, and that they may come to know the truth (2 Tim. 2:22-25, Phillips).

Knowing that Timothy would be faced with many big problems, Paul wanted to encourage him to shut out negative influences, accept positive ones, and in turn learn to be a good counselor himself one day. I have found it helpful to use his statement as the basis for a sort of self-test of my receptiveness to good counsel and capacity for positive decision making. Here are some questions based on Paul's words that I can ask myself in a given situation:

1. Do I really want what God wants in this decision, according to what I have come to know about God through prayer and the Word?
2. Am I using my energies in a positive way? Am I choosing goodness, integrity, love, and peace?
3. Is there a part of me that just loves a good fight? Do I view myself as a moral crusader; am I just trying to prove something?
4. Am I surrounding myself with positive reinforcement? Do I choose to keep company with persons who call out the best in me? Do I keep around me persons who are themselves pressing "toward the mark for the prize of the high calling of God in Christ Jesus"? (3:4)
5. Do I really believe that God is at work in my

choices, and that He can be trusted?

This little test helps me work with my attitudes and prepares me to be more open to good, godly advice, while helping me screen out advisers and advice that would drag me down. It helps me to recognize my own blind spots and alerts me to blind spots in the viewpoints of others.

But where does good advice come from? If we want positive personal reinforcement, an accurate objective viewpoint, and wise counsel, what do we look for in a friend and adviser?

Most of us would agree that "when a good man speaks, he is worth listening to, but the words of fools are a dime a dozen" (Prov. 10:20, Living Bible). Advice is certainly not hard to find. It is perhaps the one thing that most people really think is "more blessed to give than to receive"—and just because it comes from someone who's been around a long time doesn't necessarily make it good advice. In an adviser, "old" and "wise" aren't always synonymous. La Rochefaucauld once said, "Old men are fond of giving good advice, to console themselves for being no longer in a position to give bad examples." Time tends only to intensify what we already are. Age will make a good person wiser, but time can also make a fool more foolish.

All of us, old and young, seem to enjoy giving advice, and sometimes those of us who take it are not very discriminating about where it's coming from. Harry S. Truman one time quipped, "Everybody has the right to express what he thinks. That, of course, lets the crackpot in. But if you cannot tell a crackpot when you see one, then you ought to be taken in."

I remember something that happened when I was a little girl growing up in my father's church. There was a trustees' meeting after the Sunday night service. We children who had fathers on the board passed the time waiting for our dads by playing "Blind Man's Bluff" and "Mother, May I" in the church parking lot. This particular week, one of the families had traded their old car for an almost-new Buick. It was the fanciest car any of us had seen and was rumored even to have a cigarette lighter. Since few of us had ever really seen a lighter work, our friend invited us all to crowd into his family's Buick and see the lighter turn red. We waited eagerly as he explained that it would pop out automatically as soon as it was hot. As soon as it did, he waved the glowing lighter through the darkness for us all to see. Feeling a little tinge of jealousy rise inside myself, I said, "Put it against your nose." Eager to demonstrate the prized equipment, he did what I advised without thinking his action through to its logical conclusion. For weeks he wore a small brown brand on the end of his nose as living proof of his choice to take ill-considered advice.

Advice is easy to get and may come to us from people with many motivations. Our motives in listening to and acting on the advice we are given may vary widely, too. Cheap advice and wise counsel are two different matters. So the big question is—how can we tell the difference between the two, and how can we select friends and advisers who can counsel us wisely as we attempt to make right decisions?

All of us are influenced by the people we are with. Perhaps we don't think of our friends as "advisers" or "counselors," but it is very likely that they are helping to shape our thinking and outlook if we spend much time with them. Coleridge said, "Advice is like snow; the softer it falls, the longer it dwells upon, and the deeper it sinks into the mind." Most of us would pick a professional counselor carefully, yet sometimes we don't give much thought at all to the relationships that mold our thinking. Young people, especially, sometimes float thoughtlessly into entangling relationships just because of proximity or convenience; they are influenced tremendously without even being aware. Most of us have at one time or another taken advice from chance acquaintances and happenstance peers for no better reason than our secret hunch that they will tell us what we want to hear or confirm the course we want to take. This spells danger.

Just as children come home from school with the walk, the talk, the slang, and mannerism of the latest "best friend," so we adults, more often than we like to admit, pick up the thought processes, the values, and the standards of those with whom we choose to spend our time. Paul told Timothy to surround himself with people and experiences who would exert influence on him for doing right. This is sound advice for us. Our own lives will be enriched as we surround ourselves with Christian friends who are committed to spiritual growth. We must *choose* not to let the world "squeeze [us] into its own mold, but let God remold [our] minds from within" (Rom. 12:2, Phillips).

Here are some qualities to look for in a friend and adviser. These qualities also apply to us if we want to *be* the sort of person who can be taken seriously as a friend and counselor:

1. *It is important that an adviser be a person who has shown wisdom in managing his or her own affairs.* We all make mistakes and, we hope, learn some of life's greatest lessons from them. But when we are looking for a person whose advice we trust, it is important to find one who lives what he or she talks. James tells us that a person who talks one way and lives another is "double minded" and "is unstable in all his ways" (James 1:8, KJV). It is difficult to give credibility to a person who can't manage to live by his own best advice, even though his words may be true. We can always listen and consider that person's remarks— there are few people who can't teach us something— but the wisest words are lived-out words. A lived-out example is so much more effective than the empty shell of theory.

We seem to be bombarded these days with "how

to's" written by people who have "never done." Most of us are weary of people who have never raised a child telling us how to train our children, counselors who jump in and out of sleep-in relationships telling us how to make our marriages meaningful, educators who haven't spent six hours in six years with a real, live child telling us how and what our children should be taught, and social scientists who have removed themselves from the world of real, hurting persons telling us how to cure our society's ills with programs and benefits. In the Christian world, often the harshest judgments and most rigid pronouncements come from those who never had the experience. For some strange reason giving other people ten easy ways to solve their problems seems much easier when we've never had the problem ourselves. Not sharing the experience doesn't necessarily make our theories less true, but firsthand experience certainly makes us deliver our advice more tenderly and with more compassion.

In helping Timothy locate reliable leaders among the Christians of his time, Paul emphasized the importance of finding persons who demonstrated self-control, personal discipline, blameless reputations, generosity, gentleness, and compassion in teaching. A person to be followed and listened to, Paul said, should not be greedy or egocentric, and should be respected by his own family as a person of integrity. He should be a person who leads with strength and love. Spiritual leaders should themselves be willing followers of the Holy Spirit and should have a deep, working knowledge of the Word of God (see 1 Tim. 3).

Choosing to surround ourselves with friends and advisers with all those qualities is a tall order. Being that sort of person ourselves is enough to keep us busy for the rest of our lives. Yet too often we take advice on life-changing decisions from just anyone who happens along, no questions asked. No wonder we find that making wise decisions is difficult!

2. *A friend and adviser should be a person who has no ulterior motives, one who genuinely cares about our growth and well-being.* Living in our materialistic society tends to make us wary and suspicious. The first question we ask ourselves is, "What's her angle?" "What does he stand to get out of this?" To find someone who "genuinely cares about our growth and well-being" with no strings attached is indeed rare. To *be* that sort of caring person ourselves takes the work of the Holy Spirit inside our hearts.

Whenever we are getting information or advice about a problem, we need to ask ourselves, "Is this opinion colored by personal ulterior motives?" If we can find one friend whose concern is truly Christlike and genuine, we are indeed blessed! If we can resist the temptation to be a person who is anything but completely caring and genuine—even if it means personal sacrifice to help another—we are beginning to "move toward the goal of true maturity" in Christ Jesus.

We should try to avoid counselors who have become "professional Christians." I suppose we've all had the experience of trying to confide in persons whose eyes glaze over the minute we begin pouring out our hearts to them. We can just feel our "case" being sized up, categorized, and pigeon-holed in one of the neat little compartments of the counselor's experience. We can feel the person's mental machine whirring away, just like a computer, preparing to spit a premeasured prescription out at us as soon as we stop talking long enough for the insta-cure to be administered. No heart. No specialness. No real caring.

Once when I was in high school, I entered a national speech contest and needed some direction on constructing a short speech for power and impact. I wrote to a well-known minister, whom I admired for his ability to speak, and asked for his advice. This man knew my father, so he responded very warmly, giving me some helpful suggestions and wishing me well on my project. I wrote my speech, won the local contest, and finally went on to win at the state level. The prize was a trip to Washington, D.C.—an enormous thrill to a kid from a tiny town who had never stayed in a big hotel or flown on an airplane or met the president of the United States!

Some time later I saw the man who had advised me and rushed up to him, eager to express my gratitude and excitement. I introduced myself, reminded him of our correspondence, and told him I had won. He responded very professionally but without a glimmer of sharing my excitement. He seemed cordial but showed no real caring. I finished the conversation as quickly as I could and went my way greatly disappointed, for I realized I had been little more than an item of correspondence to him. Beyond that, I was an unimportant kid without an appointment.

In choosing an adviser we would like that person to be objective, fair, and honest, but he or she should care enough to hurt a little, too. There ought to be a willingness to get involved, not just for Christ's sake but for our sake as well. I have had the experience of being "ministered to for Christ's sake" by a few so-called Christian counselors, and I didn't like it much. I liked it a lot more when I was just loved by someone who cared about me and hurt when I hurt and laughed when I laughed—and listened to me. I don't know whether those people would call what they brought to my life "ministry" or not. I only know that when they touched my life, burdens were lifted, I thought more clearly, and I received the courage to believe in life and in myself again.

The Apostle Paul summarized the attributes of a wise counselor when he wrote, "Don't just pretend that you love others: really love them. Hate what is wrong. Stand on the side of the good. Love each other with brotherly affection and take delight in honoring one another" (Rom. 12:9-10, Living Bible). There's no "professional Christian" there—just an honorable person who dares to risk loving and getting involved and doing things "in such a way that everyone can see [they] are honest clear through" (v. 17, Living Bible).

3. *An adviser and friend should be a person who is kind and who reflects the attitudes of Jesus.* Both of my husband's two great-uncles were lovable and good, but they tended to express themselves in quite different ways. Uncle Lawrence just said what he thought, and was sometimes quick to "fly off the handle," as Grandpa used to say. Uncle Jesse was usually slower about jumping to conclusions, and was more easygoing and good-humored, always giving the other fellow the benefit of the doubt. One day at a family dinner, Uncle Lawrence was really giving it to the preacher for something he had done. He just raved on and on about how he was going to set that fellow straight, first chance he got. Finally, Uncle Jesse kind of cleared his throat and shifted in his seat and said, "You're probably right. But, you know, you can be dead right 'n' still be dead wrong." A lot of times *how* advice is given is just as important as the advice itself.

One time a woman in our church felt that her single calling was to "speak the truth!" She'd come roaring into any controversy like an armored Sherman tank to deliver the "truth." But most of the time, when the battle was over, there would be no survivors. She managed to destroy anyone who got in her way. We never found out whether the truth she delivered was as sharp as a two-edged sword or not, because the equipment that delivered the arms mowed down all the soldiers before they got a chance to try them.

It is important to watch out for advisers who delight in using their maturity, intelligence, or position to lord it over weaker persons or to minimize the personhood of someone with a problem. There seem to be people who just can't handle power, no matter how little they have. They love being the one with the answers.

When these people "witness for Christ," they seem to set the cause of Christ back ten years. They loudly bless the food in a restaurant, then proceed to chew out the waitress for some simple oversight. They block your driveway while they hand out copies of the "Four Spiritual Laws" door to door in the neighborhood. They are the ones who feel "commissioned" to tell the minister and his wife what their place should be in the church and to explain the standards of the fellowship to all the new converts. They make us feel intimidated by their graduate school verbiage or their degree in adolescent psychology, and they delight in pointing out that their children never had that problem but they've noticed yours do.

Sometimes people like that give excellent advice. It's just that it's so hard to take. They have not learned that, as Mary Poppins said, "a spoonful of sugar helps the medicine go down."

Paul wrote beautifully of the need for advisers to avoid such behavior: "Your attitude should be the kind that was shown us by Jesus Christ, who, though he was God, did not demand and cling to his rights as God, but laid aside his mighty power and glory, taking the disguise of a slave and becoming like men" (Phil. 2:5-7, Living Bible), and "Don't try to act big. Don't try to get into the good graces of important people, but enjoy the company of ordinary folks. And don't think you know it all!" (Rom. 12:16).

4. *An adviser and friend should be a person whose love gives him or her the courage to be honest, even if that means telling us what we'd rather not hear, but doing so in a way that makes us know he or she really cares.* If circumstances force us to choose between a person who gives us the blunt truth in an unpleasant way and someone who is soft and tells us what he or she thinks we want to hear, it is

far better to listen to the first. While bluntness may hurt, it will help us make a wiser decision in the long run. But even better, of course, is to have at least one friend who is loving enough to care about our feelings, yet whose love is tough enough to tell us the truth.

If our friendship with someone in need is to be authentic, we will love that person enough to share our true feeling and answer their questions honestly, even at the risk of losing their love. When I was little, I found it hard to believe my mother when she would say, "Now, Gloria, this will hurt me more than it does you." But now that I am a mother, I know she told the truth.

A true friend is one who is concerned about what we are becoming, who sees beyond the present relationship, and who cares deeply about us as a whole person. Beyond that, a true friend cares for us *eternally*. As brothers and sisters in Christ, our love and concern for each other goes beyond the human wholeness we strive for in this life—as important as that is. It also includes a deep caring for that eternal dimension to our lives made possible by the resurrection of Jesus Christ on that first Easter morning.

5. *A friend and adviser should be a positive person who believes there is a solution for every problem, and who will help us think objectively about every alternative.* There is no substitute for a friend who will believe with us that there is a solution. No matter how difficult the situation, no matter how tangled the web of obstacles, a good adviser will help us believe that there is a way, and that, with God's help, we *can* find it. Problems and decisions are hard enough. What we don't need is someone who will come in with a cloud of gloom and doom and tell us all the reasons why this situation is surely the end of the world.

John Powell writes, "Sometimes it seems to me that there are two kinds of people. There are those who feel obligated to tell us all the things that can go wrong as we set out over the uncharted waters of our unique lives. 'Wait till you get out into the cold, cruel world, my friend. Take it from me.' Then there are those who stand at the end of the pier, cheering us on, exuding a contagious confidence: 'Bon Voyage!' "[2]

When we get up in the morning, we have just so much energy. We can spend that energy creatively, seeking positive solutions, or we can spend it dragging ourselves down with negative thinking. Either way, we may still be tired at the end of the day. But in the first instance, we will have accomplished something and made progress. In the other, we will have plodded along and managed to make ourselves not only tired, but depressed as well!

Half the battle in solving problems is our attitude. We are not just pumping ourselves full of sunshine when we say, "Think YES!" How we think about a situation usually dictates the course we will take—and sometimes, when we get bogged down in all the tangle of detail, we need a friend who will help us think clearly about all aspects of the situation, refocusing our attention from the obstacles to the possibilities in striving for proper choices and desired goals.

I have a necklace that is made of several tiny, long chains. When I travel, I often take it because it seems to go with everything. The other day, I opened my jewelry case to find the necklace hopelessly tangled. I worked and worked with it but seemed to be making little progress. Finally, late for a breakfast appointment, I took the necklace along and continued my attempts at unraveling it on the elevator and through the hotel lobby. When I found my place at the table, I was so frustrated that I was ready to give up. One of my friends at the table said, "Here, let me do it. I love to fiddle with puzzles while I work." Viewing the necklace as a game and not a frustration, he had it untangled in just a few minutes.

My friend is a good problem solver, too. Sometimes,

I think he even creates obstacles just so he will have the joy of leaping over them. He seems to be intrigued by problems—always optimistic, always convinced that there is a solution. He almost acts as if problem solving is one of life's little pleasures, as if obstacles are there just to test his wits and make the game more interesting. Everyone needs a friend like that!

In decision making, as in most important endeavors, it is no sign of weakness to ask for help. In fact, it is the wise and mature person who recognizes his or her limitations, seeks wise counsel, and is capable of using it to find answers. In solving problems and making decisions, we certainly need all the insight we can get.

Bill and I consider ourselves very blessed to have had many wonderful advisers along our path. Whenever we have faced hard decisions, they have been there, not only with good vision and wise insight, but also with real honesty and caring. Some have had the special gift of objectivity. Others have acute insights into the long-range effects of the various alternatives. Still others know in an unusual way the power of prayer.

One such person is our friend Ione Craig. Ione came into our lives as a teacher for Suzanne's kindergarten class. We had met her at the school, but our first real contact with her came by way of a note she had pinned on our daughter's sweater one day when Bill was late picking Suzanne up from school. "Dear Mr. Gaither," the note read. "You have been late picking up your daughter several times. Perhaps you are not aware that the kindergarteners are dismissed at 11:20. It is very upsetting for your child to walk out to the sidewalk, only to find no one is waiting to receive her and she must return to the school to wait alone. From now on I will expect you to be here promptly at 11:20."

We loved it! Bill was on the school board at the time, and we considered ourselves involved members of the school community. All that made no difference at all to Mrs. Craig! She cared for Suzanne, and if Suzanne was upset, she was upset. Bill went straight to school to meet this teacher who cared so much.

Ever since that day Ione has been special in our lives. She never tells us anything just because it's what we want to hear. She thinks straight, she speaks honestly, and she believes more than anything that prayer changes everything. Many times Ione has come to walk with me beside the creek while I ask her advice on some knotty problem. Together we have prayed on the old wooden bench. She advises—gently and in love. But I thank God for her most of all because she gives it to me straight.

Friends like that are of inestimable value in our lives, But it is good to know that, even when a reliable human friend cannot be found, we have a Friend "who sticks closer than a brother" (Prov. 18:24, Living Bible). One who can accurately see all sides of the problem, One who loves us with no strings attached, One who is always at work for our good when we love Him. One who can always be trusted to give us wise counsel.

Psychologists tell us that we tend to become what the most important person in our life thinks we are. It is wonderful to know that when Jesus is that "most important person," His opinion of what we can become can shape the direction of our decisions.

FOR WORK AND DISCUSSION

Ask yourself:

1. Am I considering other viewpoints in this problem? Am I actively seeking to broaden my view?

2. Do the persons I choose to advise me
   —show wisdom in managing their own affairs?

—have no ulterior motives?
—genuinely care about my growth and well-being?
—show kindness and reflect the attitudes of Jesus?
—have the courage to be honest, even if it means telling what I'd really rather not hear?
—advise me in such a way that I know they really care?
—show a positive attitude and believe there is a solution to be found for every problem?
—help me to think objectively about every alternative?

3. Am I teachable? Do I really listen objectively with an open mind to wise counsel, even when it contradicts my preconceived ideas? Am I willing to grow and stretch?

---

1. John Powell, *Fully Human, Fully Alive*. (Allen, Texas: Argus Communications, 1976), 10.
2. Powell, 18.

8

Asking My Motives
Some Hard Questions

We can justify our every deed but God looks at our motives.
—Proverbs 21:2, Living Bible

A good man produces good deeds from a good heart. And an evil man produces evil deeds from his hidden wickedness. Whatever is in the heart overflows into speech.
—Luke 6:45, Living Bible

One day in a Bible study I attended, the group got into a discussion about motives. We were looking at the scripture, "Man looketh on the outward appearance, but the Lord looketh upon the heart" (1 Sam. 16:7), and the point was made that why we do a deed is more important than the act itself. Someone else mentioned that it is possible for us to do something that seemed admirable to others but to do it from motives that are selfish and possibly even wrong.

Throughout the discussion one young woman seemed uncomfortable. Finally, she threw down her Bible, stood to her feet, and shouted, "I don't want to hear it! I'm tired of thinking about *why* I do everything. I want to do what I want to do, and I don't want to be always asking why I did it. If I do something nice for somebody, why does it matter, anyway? Always asking why is too much trouble. I don't want to think about it!"

I'm sure each of us has at times felt just as she did. It's hard work to analyze and understand our motives. Being honest in this way puts us on the spot. Sometimes it deflates our ego, especially when our feelings of self-esteem have been pumped up by the acclaim of others. Being honest is usually a painful process, for such self-evaluation requires that we find the courage to look deep inside ourselves, to see what God sees, and then admit to ourselves what we really are.

The story is told of Robert Redford being spotted in a hotel lobby by an ardent fan just as he was walking toward the elevator. The woman rushed up to him and burst out enthusiastically, "Are you . . . are you . . . the real Robert Redford?" Redford, now inside the elevator, reportedly turned to the woman and, as the door closed between them, he answered, "Only when I'm alone."

What each of us *really* is surfaces when we are truly alone with ourselves. When all the opinions and impressions others have of us are dismissed, when all the conjecture and suppositions are peeled away, when all the surface appearances are discarded—when we stand without defense or pretense alone before God—that is when what we really are stands up. If we don't like what we see then, no amount of deception can sell us a bill of goods about ourselves. No matter how well we have fooled others, when we close the door and are alone with our decisions, our motives will outshout any good impression we might have made on others.

Actually, no one else really knows whether a decision we have made was a right one or not. There are times when a decision seems to be a big mistake to those who don't know our motives. At other times people may be very complimentary of a decision that, deep inside, we know wasn't particularly noble. In each of our lives there are decisions that we alone can make. In the final analysis, we make those decisions out of the resources at our disposal. Only God truly knows our deepest needs and our deepest motives.

Let me mention once more the prayer of the psalmist as he invites God to reveal to him what He sees: "Search me, O God, and know my heart; test my thoughts. Point out anything you find in me that makes you sad, and lead me along the path of everlasting life" (Ps. 139:23-24, Living Bible). God knows our hearts, our minds, our intentions, and our retentions— the things we are holding back. God knows us whether or not we ask Him to, but consciously asking Him to "search our hearts" requires a certain openness on our part—a willingness to come to grips with what He might show us about ourselves. It takes courage to face the things in ourselves that might be wicked or deceptive, the things that disappoint the Lord and break His heart, but our willingness to be honest with ourselves is the first step toward recognizing eternal values and living as if those were the things that really matter.

Before making any decision as Christians we might first ask ourselves: "What is my number one motive? Am I really seeking 'the path of everlasting life?' " As we saw in Chapter 2, in most decisions there are a number of goals we might hope to achieve. Perhaps we want an advancement or a better life for our families. Or we may be trying to resolve an unbearable conflict in our lives. Or perhaps we are trying to decide whether or not to move, to buy something, to resign an office, to discipline a teen-ager, to go back to college, to quit a job. Whatever the decision, the first question to ask our motive is this: Ultimately, do I really want "the path of everlasting life" more than anything else? Am I considering the eternal consequences in this decision, and do I want what God wants more than what pleases me? Am I blinding myself to what the Word of God shows me about what He is like? Do I really listen when advisers I trust point out flaws in my character that make me prefer my way or society's way or my friends' way to God's way? Am I measuring this decision by God's measuring stick?

There are times in my life, for instance, when I have been given what I truly thought was an inspired song lyric. Bill writes a tune and chords that seem to say what we both so deeply feel. Then comes the time to choose material for an album. When all of the available songs are carefully considered, our song for some reason doesn't make the final lineup.

Of course, I feel disappointed. Do I try one more time to convince the producers that this song needs to be heard, or do I take their decision as a sign that the song might be less than we thought? When others are pushing so hard to get their tunes on the album, should we push harder, too? This is where I must ask myself, "What is my deepest motive?" Somewhere I have to find the "path of everlasting life" in this matter. Does God need me to strong-arm His message? On the other hand, should I sit quietly by, refusing to invest any energy in communicating a message He has entrusted to me? Either way, what is my attitude if I fail? if I succeed?

The second question we might ask our motives is, *"Am I thinking honestly concerning material gain?"* There is something so human about greed. It comes in many shapes and sizes and disguises and almost never looks to us like the ugly ogre it is. Material gain can wear a religious habit, a mask of humanitarianism, or the new garb of self-esteem. It can look like a benefit for our children or a concern for our aged. Of one matter we can be certain: the thirst for material gain will cloud our vision and distort the truth.

In the matter of having a song recorded, for instance, I know that if a song is recorded, eventually there may be some financial compensation. If that were not so, no artist or writer could spend his or her life creating, just as ministers could not spend their full time for the work of the church. The question for me, however, becomes this: Deep in my heart, is financial gain my primary motivation? Am I spiritualizing my motive and disguising it as ministry, when in fact I can't see the value in other people's work because I'm blinded by the possibility of income. I'm sure each of us could ask ourselves similar questions in our particular set of circumstances.

Jesus knew what a problem it would be for us to think clearly about financial gain. In the Sermon on the Mount He allotted a sizable amount of attention to this problem. Instead of spending our energies unwisely by being preoccupied with material possessions, Jesus said, we should spend our lives trying to enrich ourselves spiritually, for only spiritual wealth would survive this world. Knowing how difficult it is for us to be honest about our motives where material gain is concerned, He said, "If your eye is pure, there will be sunshine in your soul. But if your eye is clouded with evil thoughts and desires, you are in deep spiritual darkness. And oh, how deep that darkness can be! You cannot serve two masters: God and money" (Matt. 6:22-24, Living Bible).

Perhaps the most deceptive trick of Satan in this regard is to convince us that the "end justifies the means," that it is all right to cut moral corners to finance a "spiritual" project. Unfortunately, this sort of faulty reasoning has been used at times even in the church. Offerings have been taken for the expressed purpose of supporting a visiting speaker, musical group, or drama team; then, when the amount exceeded expectations, part of it has been secretly kept for a worthy church project or debt. Attractive, heart-rending, or controversial projects have been invented to hype fund-raising drives for so-called Christian radio or TV "ministries." Stories have been embellished or needs exaggerated to create a more emotional climate for precipitating donations. Music has been photocopied, words plagiarized, and copyrighted materials mimeographed to avoid the cost of creative resources.

In our personal lives we are sometimes tempted to shade the truth about our life-style to make ourselves appear to be more "spiritual," instead of changing our habits so that our lives can openly speak for themselves. There may be occasions when we may be tempted to cheat our employer of time that we owe him in order to attend a Bible study, to do a good deed, or to discuss a "spiritual problem" with a fellow worker. Or we may compromise our honesty in reporting income to the IRS because we have used so much money to help someone in need or have bought gas for running errands for the church.

No wonder Jesus warned us to beware the spiritual traps of phony righteousness. He said true goodness comes from the goodness of a purified heart. Just looking good to others doesn't mean a thing if our actions are tainted by selfish and materialistic motives (see Matt. 23). Jesus' most severe judgments and scathing pronouncements were directed at the so-called religious leaders who used God's cause as a smokescreen for shoddy living and dishonest motivations.

While the thirst for financial gain is not in itself a healthy motivation for our decisions, we may find that wise decisions do result in financial gain. God has given to some the gift of being able to generate income. Their wise financial decisions provide funds needed to carry on necessary work of Christ in this world. It is worth noting that the often misquoted verse in 1 Timothy actually says that "the *love* of money is the root of all evil" (1 Tim. 6:10 italics added). The *love* of money is greed and avarice. Money itself is neither moral nor immoral. Our attitude toward it is what reveals our values.

We might also note that one doesn't necessarily have to *have* money to *love* it. Nor is it necessarily true that those who have it love it. I believe it is possible for a person to spend his or her whole life creating and managing finances and be, in that work, a devoted and useful servant of God. It is on our attitude toward financial gain or loss that the biblical emphasis falls. Affection for money will certainly fog our view, but right thinking about money, a pure commitment to Christ, and a deep desire to keep material possessions in their proper perspective can make money management a sanctified and honorable ministry to the kingdom of God and to the world. By the same token, poverty is not necessarily virtuous. Neither is it shameful. The trick is to hold all things with an open hand and to manage whatever we're given "as unto Christ," seeking always "the path of everlasting life."

R. G. LeTourneau, inventor, business executive and owner of the well-known LeTourneau earthmoving equipment companies around the world, spent his life and his enormous wealth finding ways to serve God with what he had been given. An outspoken Christian, he seemed always to view his ability to generate income as a trust from his heavenly father, a trust he had to treat responsibly and use with wisdom. It was his money—or, as he would say, God's money—that built at least two huge agricultural missionary stations in Liberia and established the LeTourneau Foundation, through which he gave ninety percent of his personal earnings, besides a portion of his company's stock, to help young people prepare for Christian missionary work.

Our friend Mary Crowley, founder and president of the well-known Home Interiors and Gifts, Incorporated was another person who spent her life finding astoundingly creative ways to use the abundant financial resources she had been given to invest in enterprises of eternal value. Besides her uncanny ability to put her money where the needs were, her infectious, simple, childlike faith in God and belief in what He can do with regular people caused hundreds to regain their self-respect and to recognize and use their own God-given potential.

The third question we might ask our motive is this: *"Am I responding to peer pressure or public opinion?"* Being motivated in our decisions by what everybody else thinks is a risky way to go. I am reminded of what Huckleberry Finn said when trying to make up his mind, "Ain't we got all the fools in town on our side? And ain't that a big enough majority in any town?"

Just because everybody else thinks a thing is so doesn't make it right. There was a time when "everybody" thought the earth was flat. No one knows how much sooner the new world might have been discovered if all the explorers had not based their decisions about charting a sailing course on what "everybody" thought. There have been times in history when "everybody" thought that tomatoes were poison, that the sun revolved around the earth, and that babies would be "marked" by their mother's prenatal experiences. Today our prisons and mental institutions are "home" to persons who took advice from "everybody" around them who said LSD would expand their minds and bring a spiritual encounter with God, that they wouldn't get caught stealing a car at night, and that it was a good idea to take along a loaded gun "just to scare" whoever tries to stop them.

Countless teen-agers have chosen to drink heavily, smoke pot, have sex—even have babies—because "everybody" said it was the thing to do—and more than we like to admit, all of us are guilty of checking the social or spiritual barometer of public opinion before we plan our pilgrimage.

Too many children come home from school to an empty house because "everybody" gauges a woman's self-worth by the job she holds outside the home. Too many men become alcoholics because "everybody" knows business deals are best cinched over cocktails. Too many children are unable to concentrate for more than two minutes at a time because their once-alert minds have been conditioned and sedated by the television programs "everybody" watches. And too many grandparents sit alone in nursing homes while a lifetime of valuable wisdom deteriorates into senility because "nobody" can live at today's pace and keep old people around the house.

What "everybody" thinks is often at cross-current with what God thinks or what we should think. The silent pressures of the society in which we live push and shove at us in every decision we face. We simply cannot afford to respond to that pressure like zombies. We who claim to be God's people must exercise moral muscle in our decision making.

This means that, in many situations, we will be in the minority; the morally courageous always have been. Jesus said we would be the salt of the earth. Nice thought. But He also implied that there won't be much of it. A little salt changes the taste of everything, but the whole world will never be salt. He said we would be the light in the darkness. Nice thought. A small light can be seen a long way off. But He was also implying that we will be shining brightly . . . alone.

Good choices are never going to be the norm. Most people won't bother to make conscientious, well-thought-through decisions. Many of those who do will not share Christian values, and so, although their logic may be sound, they will be starting from the world's premise and therefore arriving at the world's conclusion. We are to be different, chosen, unique, "peculiar," and *we will often be alone.*

DECISION VISION

It's never been easy;
He never said it would be.
The world all around us
Denies what we see.
Upstream to the current
Uphill all the way
Yet Jesus promised and signed with His blood
To give strength for today!

There's no denying the road will be rough
The journey is long and demands will be tough
But we're not tricked by what foolish men say:
If life is worth living, there's no other way.

We, too, have promised
To be His alone,
Secure in His unfailing promise
To care for His own.[1]

When it's all said and done, we stand alone before
God to make our decisions. We alone shall be accountable. Our job is to obey God in establishing our
personal priorities—and on the basis of those priorities,
we ultimately have to make our choices.

There may even be times when we feel pressure to
conform to so-called religious opinion. Well-inten-
tioned persons may try to apply their own ideas and
suppositions to our lives. This sort of pressure may be
the most difficult of all to deal with, but in the end
each of us is accountable to God alone.

In our experience, Bill and I have had to deal with
pressure from people who want to tell us what we
ought to do with our time. For instance, at this time
in our lives we have felt directed by God to invest our
time according to the following system of priorities:
(1) our commitment to Christ, (2) our marriage, (3)
the emotional and spiritual support of our children
and the enrichment of our home, (4) our writing, (5)

our recording and publishing, (6) our concerts and personal-appearance ministry. Many times we have felt intense pressure from well-meaning Christians to do what they think we should do. They might call us and say they have prayed and are sure God wants us to sing or speak at some gathering. Usually the event is worthy and something in which we would enjoy participating—but in the light of what God has given us to do, we feel it is not the best use of our time and energies.

We have to explain that we have limited our traveling because of priorities one through five and are already committed to as much as we feel God is pleased with. Most people are understanding, but sometimes there are those who are unreasonable, angry, and judgmental. Sometimes these well-meaning people use creative pressure tactics to make us feel guilty, sorry, and confused. Often we have to go back to our knees and ask God to reaffirm for us what His plan is for this moment.

In the end, Bill and I will stand before God alone to give an account of how we have chosen to use our time, our abilities, and our resources. As parents, we will give an account of the spiritual care and nurture of our children. It is we who must remember that if our personal spiritual growth is crowded out and if our marriage is pulled apart—even by "ministry"— there will be no ministry. We may be tempted to try to keep everyone happy—we want that when it is possible—but when the demands of others and the requirements of God are at cross-purposes, our choice must be to serve Him, even if we stand alone in that choice.

The next closely related question we might ask our motive is this: *"Would I choose "right," even if it appears to be occupational, financial, or social suicide."*

A popular "gospel" is being perpetrated just now that I believe is false and damaging. It is that if we choose to serve God, we will be free from pain, healthy, wealthy, wise, and trouble-free. It implies that we can recognize God's "blessing" by job promotions, increased income, big cars, grander homes, and elevated social standing in the community. This "gospel" implies that serving God really "pays," and that God wants His people to "have the best." Accordingly, the churches God is "blessing" can be recognized by the fact that they are building bigger buildings and drawing bigger (and richer) crowds. Conversely, this persuasion tends to put under suspicion those who do not prosper materially or are not healed of illness or suffer tragedy as "having secret sin in their lives."

But Jesus never said that His Kingdom would belong to the rich and powerful, the healthy and influential. Rather, He promised it to those who are persecuted for righteousness' sake, to those who are humbled by the realization of their deep spiritual need, and to those who chose to trust as simply as a child does. He said the way of the cross would cost us everything, would cause us to lay down our very lives. It would demand that we walk away from the values of this world. Jesus insisted we cannot measure the stature of the spirit by the earth's yardstick.

The lives of Paul and Job, Peter and Daniel, Timothy and John the Baptist do not indicate that right choices guarantee a trouble-free, affluent, and socially prominent life. For God's people then, and for God's people now, choosing right may mean danger, risk, loss, loneliness, and pain. Choosing right may mean that we have to take a lesser job, move to a less desirable location, and be misunderstood or even ridiculed. While it is true that society often values persons of honesty and integrity, there can well be times when those very virtues may lay our necks on the line. While fidelity, clean-living, sobriety, generosity, and truthfulness are usually the cords that bind families close, there may be times when these values may "set a man at variance against his father, and the daughter against her mother, and the daughter-in-law against her mother-in-law" (Matt. 10:35).

We are commanded, "If it is possible, as far as it depends on you, live at peace with everyone" (Rom. 12:18, NIV), but we must do so while walking "worthy of the vocation wherewith [we] are called" (Eph. 4:1). Jesus' commitment to right took Him to a cross, and He himself reminds us that "the servant is not greater than his lord; neither he that is sent greater than he that sent him" (John 13:16).

If we are to be God's people in making choices, we must be ready to choose "right" even if, by worldly standards, the choice makes us a loser. Abraham Lincoln once said, "I am not bound to win, but I am bound to be true. I am not bound to succeed, but I am bound to live up to what light I have. I must stand with anybody that stands right; stand with him while he is right, and part with him when he goes wrong."

The final question we might ask our motives is this: *"Once I have made a right choice for the right reasons, do I resist the temptation to feel superspiritual and self-righteous?"*

Every virtue seems to have its corresponding vice. Close on the heels of self-denial often comes self-pity, and the line between righteousness and self-righteousness can be fine if the Deceiver has his way.

When I was growing up in the church, I sometimes heard traveling evangelists or returned missionaries tell how much they had given up to serve the Lord, how tough the trials were, how many nights they had been away from their wives and children. Somehow it was difficult for me to hear the rest of their message. Deep inside I felt they had left something of themselves back there at the crossroads of decision. There's an old song called, "I Left My Heart in San Francisco." When I hear it sung, I always have the feeling that the person who wrote it eventually went back to San Francisco, because, even though she'd chosen to go somewhere else, she left the most important part of herself behind.

My parents were about thirty when they became Christians. Soon afterward, they felt called to the ministry but had no formal training. They found a Bible college in Florida, quit their well-paying jobs, sold their house, and left Battle Creek with an old two-wheel trailer full of portable possessions. They set up housekeeping in a tiny house (Evelyn was twelve; I was two), and Daddy worked his way through school doing carpentry work. When they returned to Michigan, they again found good jobs and started over to save to buy a house and buy the necessities. Just when they were getting back on their feet, a little church called them to help out while they were without a pastor. Eventually, my father was asked to be the full-time pastor there, but the church was small and the parsonage in bad repair. They once again sold the farm they had bought and eventually used up all the money to repair the parsonage and supplement their meager income.

At the time I was growing up in this home, I never knew we were poor. My mother made me beautiful clothes out of whatever she could find with such skill that I always felt confident and well-dressed. Our home was decorated with simple elegance because of Daddy's handiwork and Mother's art. We loved each other and always had something to share with the steady stream of company that filed through our house.

I don't ever remember my parents recounting the "trials" they'd been through or longing for the lovely possessions they once had. I did hear them give thanks over and over for the wonderful way God had led them and for bringing them from the shallow life they had lived into the wonderful "riches of Your grace," as Daddy would say when he prayed. They never bragged about their great sacrifice. Indeed, I never knew what "sacrifice" meant, because I always felt so fine and so loved.

Since I've grown up, I've come to appreciate many of the choices those two people made. I've also come to realize the beauty of the way they made their choices and just went on ahead—being and doing and giving—without feeling holy or put-upon.

When we are tempted to play the martyr about the sacrifices we make, recalling Jesus' instructions to his disciples about fasting is helpful: "When you fast, declining your food for a spiritual purpose, don't do it publicly, as the hypocrites do, who try to look wan and disheveled so people will feel sorry for them. Truly, that is the only reward they will ever get. But when you fast, put on festive clothing, so that no one will suspect you are hungry, except your Father who knows every secret. And he will reward you" (Matt. 6:16-18, Living Bible).

Once we have made a decision that is right and have made it for the right reasons, then the rightness of it will be its own argument and defense. People might come to a pity party once, but they don't like to be invited back. Rehashing again and again our sacrifices and self-denial erodes our own victory and obscures our virtue in the eyes of others.

Little children are cute when they say, "I was really good, today, wasn't I, mommy?" But it is not cute when we who are supposed to be mature boast (even to ourselves) about the things we gave up to follow Christ or the sacrifices we made to help our kids or the times we volunteered to step aside to make room for someone else in the church. Such an attitude is a sure symptom of an unhealthy motivation behind a decision, even though the decision itself might be a good one.

Motives are of utmost importance. It is hard, sometimes, to be truly honest about our motives. It is difficult to really know ourselves, for "the heart is

121

deceitful above all things, and desperately wicked" (Jer. 17:9). Only God really knows us through and through, and only He can purify us clear down to the depths of our motivation. We need His help to discover our own true identities, and to do this we must open ourselves daily to His scrutiny, again inviting, "Search me, O God, and know my heart; test my thoughts. Point out anything you find in me that makes you sad, and lead me along the path of everlasting life" (Ps. 139:23-24, Living Bible).

FOR WORK AND DISCUSSION

In this decision, ask yourself:

1. Am I really seeking the "path of everlasting life"?

2. Am I thinking clearly about financial gain?

3. Would I choose right even if it appears to be occupational, financial, or social suicide?

4. Am I resisting the temptation to feel superspiritual or self-righteous about my moral courage? Am I feeling sorry for myself?

5. Would I really dare to invite God to scrutinize my motives and reveal them to me? to others?

---

1. "It's Never Been Easy," lyrics by Gloria Gaither. © Copyright 1982 by Gaither Music Co.

9

The Waiting Place

Wait on the Lord: be of good courage, and he shall strengthen thine heart: wait, I say, on the Lord. —Psalm 27:14

Part of the creative decision-making process is *waiting*. For me it is the hardest part of all. Patience has never been one of my big attributes. By nature, I am the kind of person who talks now and thinks later. When something needs to be done, I want it done *yesterday*! I love instant soup, instant replays, and Instamatic cameras. I hate standing in line, waiting for bread dough to rise, and fishing when the fish aren't biting.

I don't think I'm the only one who finds it hard to wait. We all live in a hyped-up, revved up society. Just staying alive these days can leave us out of breath. Most of us tend to think that "waiting" and "wasting time" are synonymous. We feel almost guilty, somehow, if we don't fill every waking moment with some kind of activity for which we can see and measure results. Even our leisure time is spent racing off for the tennis court, the swimming pool, the health spa, or the skating rink. We jog, jiggle, jump, and join ourselves into exhaustion and call it "rest"—and we do it all so that we will have more strength and vitality.

But Isaiah says, "They that *wait* upon the Lord shall renew their strength; they shall mount up with wings as eagles; they shall run, and not be weary; and they shall walk, and not faint" (Isa. 40:31, KJV, emphasis added).

Over and over the Scripture tells us to do what we know to do and then to *wait*. But somehow, in the hurry and noise of our lives, it is easy to forget that we who call ourselves Christians have available to us a wonderful power. We don't make our decisions alone! The Holy Spirit has promised to "never leave [us,] nor forsake [us]" (Heb. 13:5).

After we have taken all of the active steps God's Word instructs us to take, *we have help available*! Collect all the facts. Seek wise counsel. Analyze our personal motives. Use our God-given minds and logic. After we have done it all, there are things we can know only through revelation. We can sense the witness of the Holy Spirit only when we stop to listen. We must "be still" if we want to "know."

When Moses left Egypt with a whole nation of people, he certainly had to plan ahead. Leaving Egypt was not a snap decision. Enormous preparations had to be made. You talk about organization! You talk about delegating responsibility, seeking wise counsel, and analyzing personal motives! Moses was shouldering more problems and more responsibility than any of us can even imagine! He had to know and be certain of what God expected of him. But then, after having done it all, Moses stood face to face with the biggest obstacle of all. Around him was a whole nation of grumbling, doubting, criticizing people. Behind him was Pharaoh's army. Ahead was the sea!

"No way!" we'd say. "I've prayed, studied, planned, obeyed—now this! This is the end of the line." That's just what the Israelites said, too. But Moses knew about waiting. It had taken him years of watching his father-in-law's sheep on the plains of Midian to learn about it, but by now he knew the value of being still. He said to the agitated crowd: "Fear ye not, stand still, and see the salvation of the Lord. . . . The Lord shall fight for you, and ye shall hold your peace" (Exod. 14:13-14). So they stood still . . . and they fell silent. When they were still enough for God to have their full attention, He said to Moses, "Quit praying and get the people moving! Forward, march!" (Exod. 14:15, Living Bible).

In our own decisions, there comes the time when we are face to face with the problem. It seems to be the least likely time to be stopping and waiting. But that's just what we need to do. Our limited minds can never know everything there is to know about the problem before us, but the Lord does. He has promised to give us the witness of rightness when the time comes, if we have obeyed as best we know.

There are times when that witness may contradict human logic. It didn't make sense for Moses to tell the people to march into the sea, but the order to march came *before* the order to "stretch out thine hand over the sea, and divide it" (Exod. 14:16). God alone had the whole plan. He knew all the details. Moses needed to take a moment to remember who was in charge there, a moment to relax and lie back in the trust that had brought him to the water's edge.

In our decision-making process we might call this the incubation period. We need a breath of space, a moment of silence, some time to step back from the problem and get the situation in perspective. For me, it's kind of like making a great pot of soup. I buy and prepare all the vegetables and find the right chunk of meat. I collect all the special herbs that will enhance these particular ingredients. I even pay attention to the soup kettle, because certain metals work best for certain soups. But after everything is put together in the pot and the lid is on, I turn on the heat and walk away. Even though I have done all I can possibly do to make this soup great, this is not the time to serve it up. No, there is a certain magic that can only happen when all those ingredients are allowed to simmer together slowly for a long time—something I can't make happen, something that is more than the sum of the parts.

I've known that about soup a long time, but I've had to learn it over and over in my decision making. Instead of trusting the process and waiting for the special workings of the Holy Spirit, I tend to beat the situation to death with worry and hurry trying to *make* a solution happen.

Some time ago the Gaither Trio and all the road group took a tour of Sweden, Finland, and the United Kingdom. We had never been abroad before as a group, and we didn't know how our music would be accepted there. We had been warned that it might be too "sentimental" and "family oriented" for the reserved English people, and that we were too "rock and roll" and noisy for the Swedes. In Finland and Sweden there was the language problem. Humor, especially, was hard to translate, and the cultural barrier was difficult to span.

We tried to prepare. We talked to the people and studied the different customs and special mind-sets of each region. We listened to music by native composers and read literature and poetry each country had produced, including children's stories and fables. But having done all we could to prepare ourselves to communicate the message that had driven us outside our own borders, what really made the difference was a little chorus. We never sang it in any concert. We only sang it with and to each other as the twenty or so of us rode through the countrysides from place to place. Time and time again it would begin, usually with one weary voice. Then we'd all softly join in. It became for us not so much a song as a quiet invitation to our own hearts. . . .

> Be still, and know that I am God.
> Be still, and know that I am God.
> Be still, and know that I am God.

And when we were discouraged . . .

> I am thy God who healeth thee,
> I am thy God who healeth thee,
> I am thy God who healeth thee.

When there had been a glimmer of response or thunderous applause or no response at all . . .

> In thee, O Lord, I put my trust,
> In thee, O Lord . . .

I don't know what the tour did for the United Kingdom and Scandanavia, but for all of us it was a growing time we will never forget. We may not have touched the people there, but they surely touched us! We will never be the same. The Lord taught us on that trip to stop trying so hard in our own might—to listen. In "being still" we learned to hear what the hearts of people had to say that transcended language and culture.

It is such a liberating thing to live knowing that "the battle is the Lord's" (1 Sam. 17:47). If we are truly His children, we can trust the fact that "Jesus doeth all things well." I don't "doeth" all things so well. He does! When I look back at some of the thought processes I used as a fledgling Christian to arrive at some of my decisions, I know God has to have a sense of humor and infinite patience. I was so immature, yet I wanted so much to do the right thing. It is wonderful that in God's priority system it's not by might and it's not by power but by how willing we are to listen to His Spirit. When our motive truly is to live our lives and make our choices in alignment with the mind of Christ, He will make up for what we lack.

Actually, no matter how mature we might be or how far we have come in our pilgrimage, when compared to the limitless resources of the love and knowledge of God, we are all just beginners. God honors and demands the best that we have to bring. Careless planning and slipshod choices won't get it. But even when we have exercised the best thinking of which our minds are capable and used the finest of our skills, we have still brought only our personal loaves and fishes. The problems and perplexities are too great, too complicated. Only the Spirit can move upon the broken morsels and make them adequate for the need.

Sometimes when we think we are up against a closed door, God is really at work giving us something that is "exceeding abundantly above" what we are even capable of thinking. At the time it may look as though He's giving us a no, when, in fact He's giving a YES so big we didn't even know enough to ask the question!

In the fall our family loves to go to Brown County to enjoy the southern Indiana woods while the trees are ablaze with autumn. One fall while we were there we went into the quaint little village of Nashville. One of the craftsmen who has a tiny shop there was a broom-maker. The children were intrigued with his skill at shaping the stubborn broom straws into fine brooms of every kind. We couldn't resist taking one home for the kitchen. A few days later my mother saw the broom and commented on what a perfect size it was. "That's what I want for Christmas," she said. "A decent broom!"

Now, Mother lived alone. She had a problem stomach, and it's hard for her to find food in a restaurant she could eat. Most nights she ate supper with us, but the rest of the time she didn't eat as she should because she found it difficult to cook for just one person. We all talked it over and decided that what she really needed was a microwave oven. With that she could reheat small portions of well-balanced dinners I could fix for her. She could bake potatoes and apples. She could thaw out just what she wanted from the freezer. Yes, what she needed was a microwave. So we got her one for Christmas. We hid it in the basement and covered up the big box with a blanket so she wouldn't guess.

On Christmas morning, after all the other gifts had been opened, we sneaked downstairs and brought up the big box. She opened it, all the while saying, "What in the world? You kids!" Then she saw it. She stared at it for a minute or so, then she squealed, "Why that's not a broom!" We all laughed.

Mother loves her microwave, and if you saw her today and the subject came up, she'd tell you ten reasons why you need one. Why, she can fix things she hasn't eaten in years, and so fast! She doesn't waste food like she used to! It saves her money—and she'd say, "I didn't even know I needed one!"

So often in our lives we tell God what we want, and when we don't get it just then, we think He's told us no, when the real truth is that we have asked for a broom when He wants to give us a microwave! It's not that there's anything wrong with what we've asked. It's just that our Father loves us so and knows us better than we could ever know ourselves. If we will let Him, He will give us what we really need.

My friend Lois Bock told me this experience:

At a time when financial security seemed absolutely necessary, Fred and I learned a valuable lesson in trusting God to handle our decisions. Our second child was due to arrive in four months, but we both felt God was directing Fred to resign his secure position as director of music publishing for an established company. This meant not only giving up our weekly salary, but also the company's health insurance policy. Within a few weeks Fred received an offer to work as director of another music publishing company. It seemed perfect to us. We would continue to live in southern California, and Fred would be working with friends whom he respected and admired. They met Fred's requested salary requirements. Since we had committed our future into God's hands and felt certain that our prayers for direction were being answered, we breathed a sigh of relief. We assumed that God had opened the door, so we boldly started to march through it and became excited about the new opportunities that awaited us.

At the last minute an officer of the company decided that the plan to hire Fred was not what he wanted, so he canceled all the agreements and plans. We were baffled and disappointed. "Lord, how can this be happening to us, especially now?" was my questioning prayer. I sat down in our bedroom to pray and think about this situation. Anger and anxiety almost crushed my faith in a caring, loving, heavenly Father. I again gave our future to God. We claimed the verse "My God shall supply all your needs," and began daily to exercise our faith in that promise. He proved His faithfulness and love to us. The baby that was on his way is now ten years old, as is our publishing company. Both have steadily grown and have brought much joy into our lives.

We are thankful to be children of a Father who loves us enough to allow disappointments and closed doors. We learned that the relationship would probably have been good had we gone with the first publishing company, but it would have robbed us of the best—which was God's plan for our lives, not ours.

God's plan is forever. So often we see bills to pay, houses to buy, businesses to manage, education to finish, and God knows these things concern us. But He sees more. He sees "forever." He knows we need "brooms," but He wants to feed us better, heal our infirmities, help us grow, and equip us more perfectly to serve. He wants to give us a microwave.

One time we were looking for a musician for our road group. We had done all the "homework" we knew to do. We had received many applications and résumés, interviewed the applicants, and talked to their references. We had prayed about choosing the right person.

All of the information we could find seemed to point to one of the applicants. He had the most impressive credentials. He seemed the most spiritual and knew all the "right" words. He came well recommended. But when we came to hiring him, we felt the check of the Holy Spirit. Instead, we felt impressed to hire another person whose credentials were good, but not as good as the first. He was not at all verbal about his faith, and even confessed to many doubts. He came from a religious background quite different from the rest of the group. He did not even prefer our kind of music; in fact, it was almost foreign to him. On the basis of the facts alone, we would never have hired him. Yet, after waiting and listening, we felt it was the choice we needed to make.

For the first year the young man seemed quiet and at times uncomfortable. But gradually he began to talk about what was happening in his life. The growth in him was amazing, and most of us have at some time come to draw upon his wisdom and spiritual strength. His musicianship developed as well, and he became one of the most skilled people in our group. He is now a fine composer and writer in his own right, making strong and creative statements about his Christian journey.

In this situation, we did all we knew to do to choose the right person, but the Holy Spirit had a bigger view. His ways were "higher than [our] ways" and His thoughts higher "than [our] thoughts" (Isa. 55:9). We were equipping a road group; He was shaping souls for eternity. How like the Lord to use someone we thought "we could help" to be the very one to teach and feed us all!

The waiting stage is not easy. Perhaps even harder yet is to recognize that closed doors are there to direct us to the open passageways that lead to greater progress. Waiting on the Lord is not *"doing nothing."* Waiting and trusting are active verbs in the Christian's decision-making vocabulary. Waiting is the important stage before insight, the vital step to illumination. It is the life-giving moment between preparation and certainty.

Dr. James Birren, professor of psychology at the University of Southern California at Los Angeles and executive director of USC's Ethel Percy Andrus Gerontology Center, calls the waiting stage "creative procrastination." "Creative procrastination," he says "is the art of waiting until a problem has taken on a shape you can deal with. . . . By temporarily putting the problem aside, it can take on a more manageable form when you're ready to tackle it again." In a study he conducted at the University of Chicago, he learned that creative procrastination allows us to gain new perspective so that we can "deal more objectively with the issues at hand."[1]

For the Christian, the waiting stage is the place where we let go and allow faith to take hold. It is not a substitute for work or an excuse for vacillation. In my life I have found it true that I am best able to exercise my faith when I can look God straight in the eye and say with a clear conscience: "Lord, I've done all I know to do. I have obeyed." It is then that peace comes, even though the matter may remain unresolved. I am His child, and the rest is in His hands. I can wait on Him to show me what further action I need to take.

In 1 John we are given an invitation to use a spiritual check-system in discerning the truth. As we wait and put some space between ourselves and the problem we face, we are asked to "test the spirits to see whether they are of God" (1 John 4:1, RSV). This is the time to ask ourselves about each alternative: "Does this ring true to the Spirit of God as lived out for us in Jesus Christ? Is this decision consistent with the values and objectives that I see expressed in the words and deeds of our Lord?" Our answers to these questions will be limited by our present knowledge and insight. But something changes when we can reflect upon what we know to be in tune with the spirit of Jesus.

I remember an old chorus we used to sing when I was a kid. It said:

Turn your eyes upon Jesus,
Look full in His wonderful face,
And the things of earth will grow strangely dim
In the light of His glory and grace.[2]

I like that. When I sing it I like to think about holding up, one by one, all the available alternatives in life's decisions, holding them up to the light that comes from Him, so that in His special light any flaws or wrong thinking, any phoniness or sham, will be glaringly obvious. My task, then, is to choose those things that show up clean and true "in the light of His glory and grace."

When I was a teen-ager preparing for my life's work, I could not in my wildest imagination have suspected that I would end up writing this book or lyrics to more than five hundred songs or communicating through music to people of many lands. I was not a singer. All I had was a strong desire to serve the Lord of my life in some way. I loved to write and enjoyed my speech classes. I was intrigued with words and ideas. I thought I might someday be a missionary to Africa. I didn't know.

I entered college with no clear answers. At the time few fields seemed to be open to young women. Not knowing exactly what would lie ahead, I decided to major in three subjects that I thought would best use my natural abilities and prepare me for all eventualities. I chose English (for communicating), French (in case I should be sent to a foreign missions field), and sociology (to help me better understand and work with people). Beyond that, all I knew to do was to study hard, do as well as I was capable of doing, and be open to what God wanted me to do.

Trying to be a good student didn't seem very glamorous to me at the time. I remember how different my romanticized idea of a far-off foreign mission service was from the reality of the boring hours I was spending learning French verb conjugations and noun declensions. The poems I loved to write had to be put aside while I spent days and weeks reading dull classical literature in endless iambic pentameter couplets and writing term papers. The excitement of someday working with people was eclipsed by dusty statistics on deviate behavior and research on role identification in some remote tribe in Samoa. Yet all I knew to do was what I *knew* to do!

One day during my junior year in college, my French professor called me into her office and asked if I would mind helping out with some high school classes in the nearby town of Alexandria. She said the French teacher had had major surgery and a qualified substitute could not be found. The assignment would last about seven weeks. Another girl and I could share the class load and work the teaching around our college schedule. We had been chosen, she said, because of our grade-point average and our dependability. Feeling pleased and honored, I agreed to take the job.

I began the first day of the second semester, "coincidentally," the same day a young man who had been teaching at another school transferred to Alexandria to teach in the English department. His name was Bill Gaither.

We met soon after I began teaching (with a little help from our match-making students) and began going to lunch occasionally. I discovered he was a Christian and was interested in literature, music, and politics. So was I. I discovered he had a crazy sense of humor. I liked to laugh. I discovered that he wanted to marry me the following December. He did.

In my effort to obey and prepare, I took all that French, and because of it I met Bill and I have, indeed, worked with people from many walks of life, cultures, and backgrounds. I guess I've used about everything I ever learned about communicating and expressing ideas—in writing, in singing, and in speaking. (I could have used so much more!)

One thing is sure. None of what I learned has gone to waste. I feel, instead, inadequate for the tasks that constantly lie before me. Looking back at my immature efforts at "testing the Spirit," I am filled with amazement at the way God has supplied ALL my needs, "according to his riches in glory by Christ Jesus" (Phil. 4:19). My heart is daily filled with praise for the continuing, confirming gift of His Spirit that goes beyond my ignorance and limited view and fills my life again and again.

I am now at another waiting place. When I look back over my life (waiting times are a good time for that, too), and see where God has brought me, I stand amazed. I see all the times when, in the most sincere and honest way I knew at the time, I asked God for a "broom," and I promised that if He'd give it to me, I'd be the best little sweeper He ever had. Then, look what He did! He gave me a "microwave."

Today I found my heart singing some words about waiting. Perhaps by the time you read this, my present waiting time will have given way to a clear and certain answer, and instead you may be at a "waiting place." In that case, these words I share with you:

> When I have no sure defense,
> I will wait on You.
> When there's no way I can win,
> I'll just wait on You.
> When the troubles that I face
> Are like an army all around me,
> And there's just no hiding place—
> I will wait on You.
>
> When I cannot change a thing,
> I will wait on You.
> When I've nothing left to bring, Lord,
> I will wait on You.
> When I find I'm at the end
> Of what I know and what I have to
> Offer You, it's then that I'll depend
> And wait on You.[3]

FOR WORK AND DISCUSSION

1. Do you feel sure that you:
   —have come to grips with the fact that decisions can't be avoided and are a natural part of life?
   —know where you want to go (have established long-term goals)?
   —have a working relationship with the Scripture?
   —are learning to communicate with (both talk and listen to) God?

—have identified and defined the specific problem you now face?

—have made an honest effort to collect and compute all the facts available concerning the problem?

—have sought and honestly considered wise counsel?

—have asked your motives some honest questions?

2. Consciously take the problem/decision you now face and put it into God's hands.

3. Make yourself walk away and leave it in God's hands until you can get some perspective and direction, that is, until some of the pieces of the puzzle begin to fall naturally into place without your forcing them.

4. Consciously open yourself to the Holy Spirit's leading; lower all your defenses and make yourself vulnerable to God and to others.

5. Make your waiting an active verb; consciously lie back in the confidence you have in God, yet stay totally alert to any signal He might send you to act.

1. James Birren, quoted in "How You Can Reduce On-the-Job Stress," *Grit*, 2 August 1981, 3.
2. Helen H. Lemmel, "Turn Your Eyes Upon Jesus," ©1922. Renewal 1950 by Helen H. Lemmel. Assigned to Singspiration, Inc. All rights reserved. Used by permission.
3. "I Will Wait on You," words by Gloria ©1982 by Gaither Music Co.

10

Dangers in "Testing the Spirits"

If we love one another, God dwelleth in us, and his love is perfected in us. Hereby know we that we dwell in him, and he in us, because he hath given us of his Spirit. —1 John 4:12, 13

How do we know if the signals we are getting are really from the Holy Spirit? When we stop to "test the spirits to see whether they are of God," how do we know that what we feel inclined to choose is, in fact, "of God?"

Many of us have witnessed cases in which this privilege of "testing the spirits" has been abused and used as a spiritual cop-out for avoiding work, planning, and responsibility. We have seen people act as if the Holy Spirit were some kind of litmus paper that, when inserted into a given problem situation, would turn pink or blue to indicate a foolproof plan of action. We have heard persons simplistically and thoughtlessly state, like Flip Wilson's comic character, that "God told me" or the "devil made me"—as if that were an excuse for foolhardily jumping into some random decision.

As conscientious Christian decision makers we

would hope, of course, to avoid that kind of erratic behavior. We recognize that the work of the Holy Spirit is not some sort of cheap hocus-pocus, that He does not zap us from on high with special privilege and excuse from responsible life-styles, personal pain, and daily discipleship. We recognize that the witness of the Spirit is not a substitute for work, discipline, and obedience but an illuminator that guides us to better thinking, more sacrificial life-styles, and wiser decision making.

The Bible teaches that one way we can learn to recognize the Holy Spirit is to remember that His plan is to help us discern the truth. The Holy Spirit does not want us to feel confused and uncertain. He did not come to play games with us; He wants us to know the right way.

It is *Satan* who brings confusion and distress and wants us to be ineffective and powerless. Satan wants to keep us from thinking rationally, to prevent us from rightly applying the Word of God to our daily lives, to make our prayers seem empty and powerless, to keep us from facing the facts, and to bring us advisers who will flatter and deceive.

In my decision making, learning to be alert to the way Satan works has been helpful for me. In any given situation, if I find myself doing the following things, it is not the Holy Spirit's work. Rather, the *enemy* of my soul leaves me

—*trying to avoid the problem rather than confronting it and seeking a right and permanent solution.* If he cannot keep me from facing up to the problem entirely, he at least tries to get me to settle for a short-term, temporary solution (Acts 5:1-11).

—*stirred up or angry* so that I can't see straight to do what I know to do and then relax in my trust in God (Ps. 37:4-9, Living Bible).

—*concentrating on the problem instead of on God and His Word for me.* If Satan can keep me overwhelmed by the enormity of the problem, I cannot begin to rationally seek facts and directions for finding a solution (Num. 13:17-33, 14:1-4 and Matt. 16:5-12).

—*rigidly clinging to my own viewpoint and holding tightly to my personal power base.* Wise decision making requires that we become open and vulnerable—open to others, open to God (Matt. 16:25).

—*collecting arguments that prove my own "rightness" and the other person's "flaws," or collecting facts that support my position and ignoring facts that support the alternatives* (John 21:15-22).

—*abusing my position, power, or freedom to impose my view or preferences* (1 Chron. 21, Living Bible, and Luke 12:48).

On the other hand, it is the Holy Spirit who gives us the courage to hope and love and risk. The Holy Spirit encourages us to clear our thoughts, to face problems squarely, and to be honest about ourselves— and it is He who assures us all along that we don't have to guard ourselves or be defensive when "the One who knows us best, loves us most."

After encouraging us to "test the Spirits," the Apostle John warns us that at times we will find our lives invaded by the powers that are against the Spirit of Jesus, the powers that are now "in the world." But listen to this! *"Ye are of God, little children, and have overcome them: because GREATER IS HE THAT IS IN YOU, THAN HE THAT IS IN THE WORLD"* (1 John 4:4, emphasis added).

We can learn to recognize the voice of the Holy Spirit by realizing that the Holy Spirit does not confuse us or require that we dispense with our minds, but makes us think and reason more clearly. The Holy Spirit does not erode our confidence, but gives us courage. He does not make us fearful and protective of our own position or ego but instead makes us willing to risk the honest and open scrutiny of our motives.

DECISION VISION

In his excellent book *A Place to Stand*, Dr. Elton Trueblood discusses how important it is that Christians learn to combine both experiential piety and intellectual integrity. He writes: "The Christian intellectual provides our best hope because he has access to both the reasons of the heart and the reasons of the head, and if he is worthy of his vocation he knows how to combine them. He can hold in one context both intellectual integrity and depth of spiritual experience, with no sense of incompatibility. In short, he can both pray and think!"[1]

All too often we see Christians who are good-hearted and sincere, but who hurt the cause of Christ by making unwise, ill-informed choices. Somehow, they have come to believe that there is something unspiritual about planning and forethought. So when they are faced with a decision, they just pray in a panic and assume that whatever happens next is God's will, even though it may totally contradict the most clear statements we have from the mind of God: His Word.

I once heard of a minister who became bored with his wife of several years. He left her and married another woman in the church. In discussing his new life, he was heard to say that he was thankful that God had the new spouse right there in the church leadership position, waiting for him all along.

Obviously, he was not getting his signals from the Holy Spirit, who would never contradict the specific Word of God. The Holy Spirit does not bypass rational integrity to direct us to break God's law and hurt the cause of Christ by our choices.

Tom and Marie (not their real names) owned a small business. After they heard a leading religious leader say that "God wants his children to have the best of everything," they borrowed heavily to finance a new home and car, even though their business was already struggling to make a profit. They enlarged the new year's stock on credit, and testified that they were "trusting God" to bless their "faith" and increase their profits even over and above their growing debt. Against the advice of their accountants, they continued to extend themselves, refusing to deal with the reality of rising interest rates and an ailing economy. Finally, they were forced to declare bankruptcy and lost nearly all they had built over the years. Their faith in God was seriously shaken, because they felt defeated and betrayed.

In 2 Timothy 2:15 we find the command to "do your best to present yourself to God as one approved, a workman who does not need to be ashamed and who correctly handles the word of truth" (NIV). This is a clear statement about our responsibility for aligning our choices with what the Word really teaches. It in no way excuses us for shoddy study habits or thought processes, and it insists that we work hard at *doing* what we are taught by our diligent study and preparation.

In my own decision making, I do so need "this mind . . . which was also in Christ Jesus" (see Phil. 2:5), because I have found my mind—the mind that is naturally in Gloria Gaither—to be very unreliable sometimes. When I am trying to sense the Spirit in my choices, I have sometimes found myself falling into what I call "spiritual traps." Here are four that I find subtle and hard to recognize:

The first is the trap of *choosing the "feel goods."* When trying to sense what is the most "Spirit-approved" way to go, I sometimes find myself choosing what best fits my comfort level or what produces a sense of religious ecstasy, telling myself that choice is the most spiritual. Each of us has grown up hearing certain sounds and experiencing certain emotions as we learned about God. The tone of a Christian home, the style of worship to which we were accustomed, the type of life-style we are used to—all of these are deeply ingrained in us. It is easy to let this childhood conditioning influence our view of what is "God's will." For example, when faced with choosing a new church home for our family or a place to live or work, we tend to pick that which feels most comfortable and to mistake that warm, comfortable feeling for "spirituality" or "what God would have us do."

Another example of this might be choosing a minister for our church. In helping to choose a person for this important position, we might ask ourselves: Do I really listen to the content of the sermons and tune in to the level of his or her commitment to serve Christ and others, or do I judge that person on his or her personal style? Am I really looking for someone who can lead a congregation to deeper commitments and a greater depth of service, or am I looking for someone who is most like what I am used to and who makes my emotions purr with what I have come, by conditioning, to define as "religious feelings."

Being honest about how much our feelings prejudice us can be disconcerting. But as I look back on my life, I can see that some of the best times of growth have come when I was forced out of the mold that was "comfortable" for me and into a new, sometimes frightening way of seeing and listening.

The second trap is the trap of *electing form over substance*. Like the first, this trap is subtle, and resisting it can shake us from our comfortable ruts. Perhaps the most glaring and extreme example I could give of this is the tragic mass suicide at Jonestown, Guyana (see *Time*, 4 Dec. 1978).

The church that Jim Jones began in Indianapolis started out as a quite typical evangelistic church. The services consisted of enthusiastic hymn singing, spirited preaching, testimony, and prayer. There were altar calls and offerings. As the "church" moved to California, then to Guyana, that form remained basically the same. But ever so gradually the substance changed. The preaching began to omit Jesus and to substitute an earthly leader. The testimonies were less and less about the power of God, and more and more about the deeds of a man named Jim Jones. Praises that were sung became less God-directed and more in praise of a human authority figure. Simple teaching became concentrated mind control.

Bill and I watched a newscast on the night before that fateful day in November. A newsperson who was in Guyana reported that he had witnessed what seemed to be a "sort of evangelistic church service." It included spirited singing, "testimony," and a "sermon" of sorts. The basic form had remained, but the substance had changed. The next day nine hundred people lay dead in the steaming jungle, victims of a manipulated mass suicide.

I must confess that at times I have found myself falling into the trap of following after form rather than substance—basing my opinions on appearance or format or style rather than actual content. I have been guilty of judging other persons or groups because of the *way* they did things, when I should have been paying more careful attention to substance—to the real central core of what was being said, or to the person's true character rather than his or her personality or charm. This has sometimes caused me to miss opportunities for finding rich fellowship with wonderful human beings—people who are committed wholeheartedly to Christ—just because their culture is different or their way of speaking unfamiliar.

Sometimes church groups may be guilty of celebrating a certain form of worship to the extent that the structure of the liturgy takes precedence over the message it was originally intended to proclaim. *How* one worships seems, in some cases, more important than *whom* one worships. This, I believe, is dangerous and makes for faulty and hurtful decision making in the body of Christ; it encourages harsh judgments against brothers and sisters on the basis of form rather than substance.

This brings me to the third trap, which is *confusing culture with theology*. I need to ask myself: Am I hung up on cultural trappings, or am I making decisions based on the central teachings of the Scripture? Not long ago a church organization with which I am familiar held an international convention in West Germany. The American congregations had long experienced close fellowship with the German churches by way of correspondence, shared help, and written dialogue, so everyone had looked forward to meeting together in person to worship and to know one another face to face. But the convention turned out to be disappointing for two "serious" reasons: the German Christians were aghast at the "worldly appearance" of the American woman, who wore make-up and stylish dress, while the Americans found it difficult to fellowship with German men who called themselves "Christians" yet drank great steins of beer with their meals. These two cultural differences eclipsed for many the wonderful truth and "unsearchable riches" the Word of God has to offer—riches that could have been shared with great joy.

Another area that has long been the battlefield for a cultural war is the field of Christian music. As new people come to Christ, they bring with them the unique cultural heritage that has produced the meaningful sounds from their backgrounds. When Christ becomes the prominent force in their lives, they try to find ways to express this vital and important experience—and music is a wonderful and powerful way to communicate what God has done in a life. But because Christians come from widely varied backgrounds, the styles they choose for expressing the emotions they feel so deeply will differ greatly.

Sadly, some persons in the body of Christ fail to listen for the real message behind the musical style and are prone to make judgments and issue criticisms that are damaging to sincere and enthusiastic new Christians. Assuming that their own musical tastes are a sort of "spiritual norm," some mistakenly confuse those cultural preferences with theological absolutes.

(True, some songs have been written that are weak and even some that contained biblical fallacy. Such lukewarm theology or outright error should be recognized. But it is important, on the other hand, to be clear about just what we are voting on and not to confuse cultural preference with theological truth.)

Bill and I as Christian songwriters have found ourselves on both sides of the argument. There have been times when songs that contained what we felt were some of our strongest Christian statements have been rejected by people who were offended by a certain instrument used in the recording or a certain rhythm pattern they felt was "unchristian." At other times, we have been held up to younger, more contemporary musicians as writers who create "inspired" music as opposed to that "worldly" contemporary music.

Personally, Bill and I tend to feel that all music is sacred, that there is something wonderfully "from God" about music. From the beginning of recorded history, praise and worship, joy and ecstasy, thanksgiving and invocation have found expression in music and song. The potential for organizing eight notes into new combinations is a challenge to the God-given creativity of the human mind and spirit. The possibilities of grouping those notes into rhythmic patterns only adds to the potential for emphasizing certain articulated syllables. That one pattern would be "holy" and another "evil," that one combination of these eight tones could be secular while another would be innately sacred seems to me highly unlikely. That one instrument creates a given tone by passing air through a channel or vibrating it through one or more reeds, while another makes the sound by using a hammer, pick, bow or hand to cause taut strings to vibrate seems to me to have very little theological significance. Indeed, the Bible vividly celebrates the wonderful variety of instruments we have available to us to amplify and articulate our praise and celebration, as well as our commitment and repentance. The important point is that we praise him! As Psalm 150 says, "Praise him with the cymbals, yes, loud clanging cymbals. Let everything alive give praises to the Lord! *You* praise him! Hallelujah!" (vv. 5-6, Living Bible).

Music is a powerful tool of communication, just as is great oratory, the graphic arts, and the written word. Anyone who has the gift of using any of these tools has the responsibility to pay close attention to the content of the statements being so powerfully made. Just as I see no reason to pronounce any one art medium (painting, sculpture, or the like) more "Christian" than another or any one form of literature (poetry, articles, sermons, or plays) the most "righteous," neither do I believe music has to fit a certain cultural pattern to be an acceptable tool for communicating the life-changing message of the gospel.

True, certain types of expression may be more appropriate for certain cultural settings. But the important point in our decision making is to be alert to any tendency we might have to make decisions about others in the body of Christ based on our own cultural preference instead of on the real content of what is being expressed. In this, as in all matters, the central commandment is one of love:

> Be gentle and ready to forgive; never hold grudges. . . . Most of all, let love guide your life, for then the whole church will stay together in perfect harmony. . . . Remember what Christ taught and let his words enrich your lives and make you wise; teach them to

each other and sing them out in psalms and hymns and spiritual songs, singing to the Lord with thankful hearts. And whatever you do or say, let it be as a representative of the Lord Jesus (Col. 3:13-17, Living Bible).

The fourth trap involved with "testing the spirits" is that of *assessing God's approval or blessing of a decision by the criteria of health, good fortune, or material or statistical gain.* We live in a materialistic society with a humanistic world view. Everywhere we are bombarded by materialistic values, by the tendency to measure success and worth in numbers. Sadly, these values have seeped their way into the Christian community.

Often people have said to Bill and me as we travel with our performance group, "My, God certainly is blessing you; I see you had twelve thousand people in Atlanta." That may be nice to hear, but that kind of flattery is dangerously deceiving. Nowhere in God's Word can I find any place that tells me God is "blessing me" if we draw big crowds, stay well, have a fine car—and if my face never breaks out! Hitler had a crowd, but that didn't make him right.

Don't get me wrong; I'm thankful that we could sing and speak to twelve thousand people in Atlanta. I wish there could have been fifty thousand, because we went there to tell people about what Jesus has done for us and what He can do for them. But just the fact that there are big numbers doesn't mean "God is blessing." And just because someone gets a promotion or builds an architectural wonder or gets more money sent in for a new TV program than the guy does on the other channel doesn't necessarily mean God is blessing or approving. And the fact that Tony Melendez was born without arms or that Joni Eareckson Tada doesn't walk doesn't mean God *isn't* blessing them! We can't measure the things of the spirit the way the world measures success.

DECISION VISION

When I am trying to sense the leading of the Holy Spirit I must learn to recognize Him because I really *know* Him through the scriptures and through personal experience. I must learn not to be sidetracked by worldly success or the lack of it.

In her wonderful little book *Leave Your Self Alone*, Eugenia Price writes: "You know there is a life-changing difference between acting in obedience to the Lord who is our personal friend—whom we know—and in having *religious feelings* that prompt us to say or think, 'Oh, I'd better trust God in this.' We *can't* trust the God we don't know personally. But once we get into the business of learning about His true nature, trust is automatic. I do not trust Him simply because I feel it's the moral or wise thing to do. I trust Him because I've learned enough about what He's like to know that only He is totally trustworthy."[2]

To avoid the traps in "testing the spirits," we must truly know God—His character and intent—through study and personal experience and through prayer and clear thinking. When trying to discover the leading of the Holy Spirit, we can be sure of this: the Holy Spirit will not lead us to do something that is contrary to God's Word and character, and He will not contradict the knowledge that He has truly revealed to us about Himself through prayer, personal experience, and the counsel of wiser, more mature Christians. He helps us not to be diverted by our own comfortable preferences, familiar forms and habits, cultural trappings, or materialistic surroundings. He gives us clear vision and keen focus on the real issues. He gives us the courage to risk vulnerability and change.

On the other hand, whatever clouds our view, encourages us to protect our own selfish interests, urges us to cling to our viewpoints, rationalizes our anger and resentments, and urges us to jump to irrational conclusions irreconcilable with God's stated Word, cannot be the Holy Spirit.

Dangers in "Testing the Spirits"

In his paraphrase of 1 Corinthians 3 and 4, Leslie Brandt puts it this way:

It is high time that we who are God's servants
    leave our milk diet of subjective ecstasy
    for the meat of basic discipleship.
We no longer have to play the numbers game.
Our great God does not judge our worth
    by human standards.
Nor should we.
We do not have to always *feel* good
    about our accomplishments
Nor should we need the ego lift of popular
    acclaim or the plaudits of our peers.
We, each one of us, have a job to do,
    and we assume our responsibilities in
    accordance and with the guidance, the gifts,
    and the opportunities that our God makes
    available to us.
As long as we are faithful to our task
    and in our witness,
    whether we lay foundations for others to
    build upon or build upon those that
    have already been laid,
    we are the workmen of God;
    and God alone knows the true value and
    effectiveness of our efforts.
The point is, our validity is not dependent
    upon visible successes.
It is granted and stated by God Himself. . . .
How important it is to relate continually
    to the value judgments of our God!
If we seriously embrace the commission of
    Christ, we cannot begin to imagine to what
    heights or depths
    our discipleship will take us.
There will be moments on the mount.
There will be hours down in the valley—

down where there is no honor or
recognition, only loneliness and
persecution, even suffering and
imprisonment, as we seek to identify with
the victims of war and poverty and
oppression and injustice,
   and to communicate the love and healing of
Christ to those who need it the most.
Whatever the rewards for faithful service
in some future dispensation,
   we are the sons and daughters,
   disciples and servants of God.
Our appointment as such is reward enough.
God grant
   that we may be loving and faithful and
   obedient.[3]

It is reassuring to know that we aren't abandoned
to muddle through the tough decisions by our own
wits alone. There is a dimension of insight beyond
raw rationality. There is a vision far greater than
eyesight. Alert to our own mind-games, we can focus
on the Divine Consciousness in which our conscience
rests. He is the Knowing beyond knowledge and the
Wisdom above the wisest of men.
   Alexander Solzhenitsyn voices our confidence in
this prayer:

How easy for me to live with You, O Lord!
   How easy for me to believe in You!
When my mind parts in bewilderment or
   falters,
when the most intelligent people see no
   further than this day's end
and do not know what must be done
   tomorrow,
   You grant me the serene certitude
that You exist and that You will take care

that not all the paths of good be closed.
Atop the ridge of earthly fame,
I look back in wonder at the path
which I alone could never have found,
a wondrous path through despair to this point
from which I, too, could transmit to mankind
a reflection of Your rays.
And as much as I must still reflect
You will give me.
But as much as I cannot take up
You will have already assigned to others.[4]

FOR WORK AND DISCUSSION

1. There is no doubt that the Holy Spirit is the ever-available helper in our decision making, but we need to learn to recognize His "still small voice." In relation to your decision-making process, ask yourself these questions:

   a. Do I expect the Holy Spirit to excuse me from disciplining myself and working to make my decisions wise and valid?

   b. What are some blind spots I might have? Do I really want the Holy Spirit to "illumine me," as the old hymn says? (Look up the word *illuminate* and discuss how the Holy Spirit's presence illuminates our decision-making process.)

   c. Do I think of the Holy Spirit as something illusive and mysterious, almost spooky? Or do I feel that He is a friend whose presence is comforting and helpful and reassuring?

2. In regard to the Holy Spirit and the specific choice you are facing, try to identify any of the four spiritual traps into which you may be falling:

DECISION VISION

a. Am I mistaking comfortable feelings (perhaps conditioning of my childhood) for the "witness of the Spirit"?

b. On which basis am I forming my opinions in this situation: substance or form?

c. Am I confusing culture with theology? (Culture refers to a particular form or stage of civilization. Theology refers to what we have come to know, through study, about God.) Which aspects of my decision am I basing on theological absolutes and which am I basing on the conditioning of my cultural setting?

d. Am I assessing God's blessing or approval by the criteria of material or statistical gain? When I say, "God is blessing," what do I mean?

1. Elton Trueblood, *A Place to Stand* (New York: Harper & Row, 1969).
2. Eugenia Price, *Leave Your Self Alone* (Grand Rapids, Mich: Zondervan Publishing House, 1979), 101.
3. Leslie Brandt. *Epistles/Now* (Concordia Publishing House, 1974, 1976). Used by permission.
4. "How Easy for Me to Live with You, O Lord!" from *Solzhenitsyn: A Pictorial Autobiography*. Editions du Sevil, 1974. English translation 1974 by Farrar, Straus and Giroux, Inc. Reprinted by permission of Farrar, Straus and Giroux, Inc.

11

It's Time to Decide

If any of you lack wisdom, let him ask of God. . . . But let him ask in faith, nothing wavering. For he that wavereth is like a wave of the sea driven with the wind and tossed. —James 1:5-6

There is a big difference between "waiting on the Lord" and plain old procrastination. The time comes when we've analyzed, prayed, studied, and waited long enough—when we must decide. Most of us have stood like Scarlett O'Hara gazing at some blazing crisis in our lives and wailed: "I won't think of it now. I can't stand it if I do. I'll think of it tomorrow at Tara. Tomorrow is another day."[1] But this is tomorrow, and our feet are as firmly planted on "Tara" as they're ever going to be. In our hearts we know a decision must be made.

Delay can devour opportunity. As Shakespeare states in *Julius Caesar*:

There is a tide in the affairs of men,
Which, taken at the flood, leads on to fortune;
Omitted, all the voyage of their life
Is bound in shallows and in miseries.

DECISION VISION

On such a full sea are we now afloat,
And we must take the current when it serves,
Or lose our ventures.[2]

Some for fear of commitment to a choice have spent
their whole lives "bound in shallows." But the amiable
tides of the open sea belong only to those who dare to
chart a course and set sail when the flood is right.
Waiting too long destroys our will to try and leaves us
defeated and pessimistic. The future belongs to those
who can decide.

Jean Mayer, president of Tufts University has said,
"In this tense, ever more crowded, ever more interde-
pendent world, decision making is becoming more and
more crucial. I do not hesitate to proclaim that the
future of the human race will depend on whether
graduates, citizens of the greatest democracy on earth,
members of the most highly developed technological
society in the world, have the wisdom and the courage
to make, and carry out, the right decisions."[3]

Not only does the future of mankind and of our
society depend on decision makers; our own personal
growth and destinies also depend on our willingness
to make decisions. It is the commitments we make
that define what we are as persons. That is why it is
so important to begin our journey as decision makers
by deciding to commit ourselves to something and
Someone bigger than ourselves. It is not nearly so
important where we've been or how capable we feel
we are. The big questions are "Where am I going?"
and "What is my primary commitment?" If the answers to those questions point to a cause bigger than
ourselves, then courage to decide will come as a natural and necessary result. If, on the other hand, our
search for identity begins and ends with ourselves, we
will in the end lose ourselves in uncertainty and
self-analysis.

The story of Jesus' invitation for Peter to walk on

the water holds an important analogy to our personal adventure as decision makers. Obviously, what Peter was asked to do was frightening—to the rational mind, seemingly impossible. No one he knew had ever done such a thing. Yet Peter's commitment was to the Person who told him, "Come," not to the project of proving that he as a human being could actually walk on the surface of the water. The limitations of his anatomy, the conditions of the environment—none of these was central in Peter's mind when he stepped out of the boat. His commitment to Jesus was his reason for choosing to step out, and, as long as he kept his eyes focused on this commitment, he did indeed accomplish something that his own limitations would otherwise have prevented.

In her book *Pathfinders* Gail Sheehy reports a study she made to determine what characterizes "high-well-being" people—people who have a strong sense of satisfaction about themselves and about their lives. One thing she discovered was that, in every group she surveyed, the most satisfied people were also likely to be the most religious. Another of her findings showed the strong role that commitment plays in shaping lives. One of the questions on her survey was, "Are you devoted to some purpose or cause outside yourself and larger than yourself?" Sheehy reports: "The majority of respondents said 'no.' Yet, the results among highest satisfaction people were dramatic: The greater well-being a person reflected, the more likely he or she was to have an outside purpose. *The distinction is so considerable as to make the current philosophy of looking out for number one sound like a national suicide pact"* (emphasis added).[4]

Many times at the Praise Gathering for Believers in Indianapolis, we have been privileged to have Anthony Compolo, a noted professor of sociology at Eastern College in Pennsylvania, as a speaker. Dr. Compolo has a great deal to say about psychology's current

ation with the influences of one's personal
;ed on his wide counseling experience and on
the changes he has seen in people's lives, however, he
has come to a different emphasis. He makes this
statement:

What you commit yourself to be will change
what you are and make you into a completely
different person. Let me repeat that. Not the
past, but the future, conditions you, because
what you commit yourself to *become* deter-
mines what you are—more than anything
that ever happened to you yesterday or the
day before. And therefore I ask you a very
simple question: What are your commitments?
Where are you going? What are you going to
be? . . .

You show me somebody who hasn't decided,
and I'll show you somebody who has no identity, no personality, no direction.

I continually meet people who say, "The
major problem of today's contemporary youth
is that they have an identity crisis!" You
know why they have an identity crisis? They
don't have a commitment! You show me a
young person who is committed to Jesus
Christ as Lord, Savior, and God; I'll show you
somebody who knows who he is and what he
is and what his life is about! And you show
me somebody without that kind of commitment and I'll show you somebody, who, [to
paraphrase] T. S. Eliot is the "hollow man,
the empty man, blown to and fro by the
wind."

We have confused people in our world, we
have confused adults in our world, because
we have uncommitted people in our world!
Commitments, in fact, define who we are!

It's Time to Decide

I firmly believe that the most important step in actually making decisions is to *establish and clearly define our commitments*. If you as a decision maker have not decided to commit your life to Jesus Christ, let me urge you to begin there before you try to handle the other decisions of your life. Without Jesus, decision making is a precarious undertaking. I believe that the big decisions of life should never be attempted unless there is first a commitment to Him. The choice of a marriage partner, an educational direction, a new job, a place of residence—all depend greatly on our primary commitment to God. Decisions about parenting, about relationships, about budgeting time and energies all depend on just what our ultimate commitments are.

In previous chapters I have already discussed vital steps in the decision-making process. But after we have done all we can to prepare for making a wise decision—including committing ourselves to God and to eternal values—we need to *decide promptly and act on our decision*. Knowing what we should do is not good enough; decisions involve action—doing what has to be done. There is nothing creative about procrastination at this point; it can only bring fear and frustration. Every moment wasted after a decision is ripe hastens the decay of our effectiveness and self-confidence. In a way, procrastination is also an act of doubt, for it tends to indicate that we don't really trust what God has directed us to do.

When I say a decision is *ripe*, I don't mean that everything about the decision will be clearly visible and the results guaranteed. If we waited until there were no risks, we would never make decisions. But deep in our hearts we know when a decision's time has come. Time spent pondering the matter beyond that moment is wasted and destructive and creates a fertile breeding ground for fear and uncertainty.

Karl Rahner puts it this way, "A man who refuses to commit himself for fear of following an insight that cannot be mathematically verified does *not* in fact remain free but rather enters upon the worst of all commitments—that of living his life without commitment. He tries to live as a neutral, deciding nothing, and that in itself is a decision."[5]

I'm sure no American can forget the agonizing year fifty-two Americans were held hostage in Iran or the incredible feeling of relief the nation felt at their release. Six other Americans owe their lives and early escape from Iran to a decisive man with a large commitment. His name was Kenneth Taylor, and in November of 1979, when the crisis began, he was the Canadian Ambassador to Iran. For three months he risked his life and the lives of his family to harbor these six Americans, who had fled the U.S. Embassy as Iranian militants were storming it. Ambassador Taylor was an intelligent, loyal man with a record of commitment to the laws of his country, yet he listened to a higher commitment to freedom and human dignity. He acted quickly and without regard to his personal safety. His decision had no guarantees except the inner confirmation of the rightness of his choice. Yet he saw his decision through and eventually succeeded in seeing the six Americans safely out of the country.

Anwar Sadat was another man whose ability to take difficult and decisive action changed the course of events at a turbulent moment in history. His commitment to peace motivated him to risk the disfavor of his colleagues and countrymen by breaking a twenty-nine-year ban on direct Arab dealings with Israel. He courageously crossed the border into former enemy territory to proclaim his willingness to "live with [Israel] in permanent peace and justice."

In writing about Sadat after his assassination, Henry Kissinger made a statement that gives insight into the character of great decision makers. "Sadat was a very great man who made the difficult seem effortless. The difference between great and ordinary leaders is rarely formal intellect but insight. The great man understands the essence of a problem; the ordinary leader grasps only the symptoms. The great man focuses on the relationship of events to each other; the ordinary leader sees only a series of seemingly unrelated events. The great man has a vision of the future that enables him to place obstacles into perspective; the ordinary leader turns pebbles in the road into boulders. . . . He [Sadat] understood that a heroic gesture can create a new reality."[6]

In addition to being sure of their ultimate commitments and being prompt and decisive about their choosing, decision makers must be able to *separate the crucial from the trivial*. Many times in this book I have mentioned priorities. Now again I find priorities important when it is time for actually making the decision, because decisions are almost never simple, one-issue problems. There are usually many facets to the choices we are called upon to make. I have found it helpful to try to weed out the side issues and scrape off the barnacles that cling to the problems. Then I can zero in on the central decision, and give first attention to the issue that first demands an answer.

For example, as a mother, I have been called upon to make decisions that helped shape my children's values. It has been important not to leave the impression with them that my personal preferences about clothes or hair styles or the influences of local culture is of equal importance with the Christian "absolutes" defined in the Scripture. As a parent I have learned to save my no's for things that really matter, and not make such a big deal out of what kind of jeans to buy or how long hair should be. I found it important to make clear statements about the real issues and not cloud the issue by making too many decisive pronouncements that all sound equal in importance. Our children needed to recognize which things were merely style and culture and which were truly issues of morality. But some days I found myself more upset about socks on the floor than about obscenities on TV. All too often I found myself sitting passively while some situation comedy told my children that "three's" only "company," yet I could lecture for fifteen minutes on how ridiculous it was that my daughter couldn't wear her full-legged jeans that "fit her perfectly well" because she felt "dumb" in them or that our son had to have hair that gave him a sense of identity.

While it is true that I have to decide about socks and jeans and haircuts, I must never forget that those in themselves aren't the real issue. The real issues are responsibility, integrity, consideration of others, and honesty. A decision must have "eternity" in it!

To committed young people, it sometimes seems that they are making a lot of negative choices, that they spend their lives saying no: no to drugs and alcohol, no to going places they feel Christians shouldn't go, no to the attitudes around them about things like cheating and cutting corners, no to premarital sex. "It seems as if all I do is say no," our teen-age daughter once said to me. Her words stuck with me all that week, and I struggled to find a way to help her put things into better perspective. The result was a song lyric that went like this:

Saying "no" may mean that I've said "yes" to something higher;
Pleasure for a season cannot buy eternity.
Joy and lasting peace and deep contentment are a treasure,
No cheap thrills or easy rides will ever trick from me.

Saying "no" to lesser men means I've said "yes" to Jesus.
I am very careful whom I choose to call my Lord.

I will gladly wash your feet or offer any service.
Bowing only to the law of love found in His
Word.
Markets of the world may bid to make me easy
barter.
But I refuse to sell myself in bits and pieces.
Noisy vendors vie for my consent with second
guesses,
But I will spend my yesses on things that never
die.

When you sense a calling that is the best that is
within you,
When you know deep in your heart you've found
a better way,
Turn your back on all the voices that would drag
you downward:
Saying "no" may be the grandest "yes" you'll ever
say.[7]

So we were back to commitment again. And that's a
positive thing, no matter how many "no's" it demands
of us.

Another important aspect of making a clear-cut
decision is to *make the decision and don't look back.* Oh, I
don't mean that we should never try to learn from
our mistakes; that kind of hindsight can enhance
foresight. What I'm talking about is going over and
over decisions in our minds, agonizing over our defeats
or gloating over our victories, worrying and fretting
over choices we have made.

For one thing, just as much time and energy is
needed to relive decisions as to make them in the first
place—maybe more. For another, it robs us of precious
energies we could spend going on to what God has in
store for us. To keep looking back, fearful that we
have made a mistake is defeating and debilitating. It
stagnates our progress and destroys our hope. Just as

surely as Lot's wife was turned into a pillar of salt when she disobeyed God and looked back to Sodom and Gomorrah, our pilgrimage will be stopped in its tracks if we give in to misgivings and uncertainty.

Here again, always looking back tends to reflect a lack of trust in God's power to help us make wise decisions. Looking ahead and spending our energies on finding new ground to conquer demonstrates our confidence in His leading.

Sometimes we will make mistakes. Because we are human, we may not always interpret God's leading perfectly. But even when we make mistakes, if our motives have been right and our decision the best we knew to make at the time, we can learn from our mistakes, trust God to help us grow, and go on.

There are some wonderful verses in Philippians about a positive, forward-looking attitude. I quote it from the Living Bible so that we can hear it anew:

> Fix your thoughts on what is true and good and right. Think about things that are pure and lovely, and dwell on the fine, good things in others. Think about all you can praise God for and be glad about. Keep putting into practice all you learned . . . and the God of peace will be with you (Phil. 4:8-9).

No decision is an isolated island in the sea of our days. Each decision we make, each bit of growing we do, brings new horizons into view. That is why a final, important part of decision making is to *accept and be willing to deal with the consequences of our decision.*

Reminding ourselves that decisions produce results is helpful. We need to be prepared to deal with those results. On the other hand, we can't always expect *immediate* results from our choices. Time is needed for some decisions to produce noticeable results. When Bill and I decided to have a baby, we didn't expect to have a mature adult the next day—one we could display as an instant outcome of our choice. In fact, we are still dealing with the surprises that keep coming to us as a result of that choice. But it's been our joy to deal with the consequences of our choice, and, by the way, that choice has brought an unending procession of new decisions to be made.

As with parenthood, most of our decisions bring some surprises, but that is what life's wonderful adventure is all about. Some of the consequences of our choices are difficult and painful; some are happy delights, but both represent opportunity for growth and joy.

Sometimes problems that require decisions of us come into our lives unsolicited. Circumstances or accident, the actions of others or situations beyond our control confront us. Some circumstances cannot be changed; all we can change is our attitude toward them. The death of a loved one, injury or illness, the loss of a job when the economy fails or our place of employment closes, the bad choices of others—all these enter our lives uninvited, yet they present us with an unavoidable choice: What will be the spirit of my response? With what attitude will I confront this problem?

We live in a General Motors town. Some years ago, the decline in automobile sales severely affected our area. Hundreds of families were out of work—so many, in fact, that NBC news broadcast a special feature on our county. We became "famous" for having the highest unemployment rate in the nation.

One family close to us was without work because the factory where the father worked had closed completely. In one year all benefits stopped, and the situation looked bleak, indeed. The family had several small children. They had no hope of finding another job in an area already overloaded with people looking for employment; the father's health kept him from being accepted for the few heavy manual jobs that were to be found.

In this seemingly impossible situation, my friend (the wife and mother) did not panic. She first thought through the problem, listing possible alternatives. Then she counted all the things of great importance that they still had. They had the Lord. They had each other. They loved each other. They had a place to be. They had healthy children. They had their ability to laugh and play. They had friends. It was summer and they needed no heat. On and on she counted the things they had that really mattered. This helped her avoid the awful strangling vise of fear and panic and gave her some space around the problem in which to begin thinking of some creative solutions.

At the time, my friend couldn't change anything. But she could choose her attitude, and her unsinkable spirit kept her family from despair. Help began to come their way from friends and neighbors, and she was able to find some part-time work to help out. All the while she insisted that God would take care of them. He did—and her strong, positive faith was an encouragement to many who were more fortunate, but not more blessed!

The prophet Habakkuk talks about our ability to always choose our own attitude, even when we cannot affect any other change: "Although the fig tree shall not blossom, neither shall fruit be in the vines; the labour of the olive shall fail, and the fields shall yield no meat; the flock shall be cut off from the fold, and there shall be no herd in the stalls: Yet I will rejoice in the Lord, I will joy in the God of my salvation" (Hab. 3:17-18).

FOR WORK AND DISCUSSION

1. The decision you are facing can be made with greatest certainty when you are certain of your commitment to

something (and Someone) bigger than yourself or your problem. Ask yourself

   a. Is anything standing between me and God that is keeping me from totally trusting Him in this decision?

   b. Am I willing to be decisive and straightforward?

   c. Am I procrastinating?

   d. Am I zeroing in on the aspects of this decision that are crucial? Am I giving too much attention to the trivial?

2. When you have made the decision, ask yourself:

   a. Am I wasting my energies rehashing and backtracking?

   b. Am I accepting the responsibility of carrying through on my decision?

   c. Am I prepared to accept and deal with the consequences of my choice?

   d. Am I willing to wait patiently for the results?

   e. What attitude am I choosing toward the things in my life that I cannot change?

1. Margaret Mitchell, *Gone With the Wind*, (New York: Macmillian, 1936).
2. William Shakespeare, *Julius Caesar*, act 4, sc. 3, lines 211-17.
3. Jean Mayer, *The Chronicles of Higher Education*, 8 November 1976, 32.
4. Gail Sheehy, *Pathfinders* (New York: William Morrow & Co., 1981).
5. Karl Rahner, *Do You Believe in God?* (New York: Paulist/Newman Press, 1969).
6. Henry A. Kissinger, "Sadat: A Man with a Passion for Peace," *Time*, 19 October 1981.
7. "Yes to Something Higher," lyric by Gloria Gaither, 1980 by William J. Gaither.

12

I Will Go On

Forgetting what is behind and straining toward what is ahead, I press on toward the goal to win the prize for which God has called me heavenward in Christ Jesus. —Philippians 3:13, NIV

S o what happens if you've blown it? What if you've made more than your share of bad choices and your life is in ruins? What if you have read this whole book shaking your head with regret that you didn't take decision making seriously sooner? "It's too late now," you might be saying. "I've already made such a mess of things."

Or maybe you've been thinking, "I know that already!" At each point you can give ten examples of the objectives you've accomplished by your clear thinking and wise choices.

Or maybe you are like me—somewhere in between. Maybe the pattern of your past decision making looks kind of like a roller coaster: some high places, some deep valleys, some slow steep climbs to a peak of sorts, some abrupt dips.

To us all the apostle writes in Philippians: Forget it! "Forget what is behind," and "press on." Paul seems to be telling us that there is no way we can "press on" with our full energies if half of our attention is focused on past failures *or successes.*

Suppose there are successes in the past. Strange as it may seem, too much attention to past accomplishments can thwart our progress as surely as dwelling on our failures. I once knew a man whose conversation was filled with boasts about his past. While it was true that he had made some noteworthy accomplishments, the world passed him by while his head was turned backward, gloating over what he had done. Because of his failure to go on studying and growing, his creativity stagnated. Finally, when he did try to make a new contribution, his ideas were outdated and weak. Instead of recognizing the problem and admitting that the work of others was better and more innovative, he became bitter and critical. His attitude eventually robbed him of the honor and respect he might have enjoyed had he continued to grow and develop an honest appreciation for the gifts of others.

Sometimes our past accomplishments can establish a high-water mark that is intimidating and makes us fearful of failure. There have been times in my life when I have found my creative energies frustrated in this way. Some years ago I was working with my husband, Bill, on a musical about the cost of discipleship. So many people asked me if this work was going to be another "Alleluia" (a popular musical we had written with Ronn Huff a few years earlier) that I almost lost my nerve. "What if we fail? What if I can't write words like that again?" These thoughts haunted me.

Finally, I had to consciously clear my mind of fear, focus on the real purpose that had made us believe so much in the need for this work in the first place, and leave the outcome with the Lord. I began to recognize that I had let other people's expectations distract me from my real goal and pull my attention to the selfish desire to protect my ego from failure.

Ironically, the musical was based on the very text I myself needed: "Therefore, since we are surrounded by such a great cloud of witnesses, let us throw off everything that hinders and the sin that so easily entangles us, and let us run with perseverance the race marked out for us. Let us fix our eyes on Jesus, the author and perfector of our faith" (Heb: 12:1-2, NIV). I asked God to give me the courage to go on risking, even if I failed. I accepted the fact that this new work was unique, like nothing else we had ever attempted, and that I didn't have to prove anything. All the Lord expected of me was to work hard, think clearly, and trust the results (or lack of them) to Him. I felt released and freed to turn my energies toward what lay ahead.

Perhaps, on the other hand, the past is haunting you because of brokenness and pain. When you think of the decisions you now face, your moral muscle turns to jelly because past failure has drained you of your confidence. You may feel as though life has overpowered you, that your broken spirit is no match for the future. The "monster of your past" may seem to hover over you like a firebreathing dragon waiting to devour any creative endeavor.

If this is where you are, there is wonderful news: YOU CAN START AGAIN! I wish I could print this in four-inch type, because these words shout at us from the pages of God's Word. They should be written by a sky-writing plane across the sky for us all to see every morning because (and now I'm whispering) we all fail. Yes! We all fail!

If we say that we have no sin, we are only fooling ourselves, and refusing to accept the truth. But if we confess our sins to him, he can be depended on to forgive us and to cleanse us from every wrong. . . . My little children, I am telling you this so that you will stay away from sin. [Now I'm

shouting again!] BUT IF YOU SIN, THERE IS
SOMEONE TO PLEAD FOR YOU BEFORE THE
FATHER. His name is Jesus Christ, the one who
. . . took God's wrath against our sins upon him-
self, and brought us into fellowship with God;
and [can you hear?] HE IS THE FORGIVENESS
FOR OUR SINS. . . . (1 John 1:8-9; 2:1-2, Living
Bible, emphasis added).
Our friend Reuben Welch puts it this way:

How beautiful that this last "if" clause
   meets us with such profound
                    and tender understanding
              of the flow of our lives in Christ.
                        His intention is clear
My little children, I am writing this to you
that you sin not . . . but if!
But if anyone does sin
      we have an advocate with the Father
      Jesus Christ, the Righteous.
We would never have had the courage
   to put that in, yet how desperately we need it.
                 Isn't that great?
                 Let's just put it this way:
My little children
my intention is
          that all marriages be happy
               and mature
               and fulfilling—
                        but if . . .

My little children
I'm writing this
        that all of you be healthy and whole
          in body and mind—
                        but if . . .

I'm writing this
       so there won't be brokenness,
             tragedies,
             scars

but if . . .
Suddenly into the realities of a fallen world
  and into the brokenness of it comes this healing
  word:
  we have an advocate.
Not at the point of our achievement,
but at the point of our failure.
  Christ the Advocate is by our side,
              on our side.
  Righteous Jesus Christ
  and He is the expiation for our sins—
not our struggles
  not our self-hate
    not our self-loathing
      nor our rash promises or vows—
He is our advocate, our way to handle our sins.[1]

When Suzanne was little she was the "project kid"
around our house. Almost every waking moment she
seemed to be painting, cutting, coloring, building,
molding, or inventing something. One day she was
creating a painting for me at her little maple table in
the corner of the kitchen. She had the picture about
half finished when she dropped a big glob of brown
paint right in the middle of her paper. I watched her
out of the corner of my eye as she tried to fix it.

At first, she tried to turn the blob into something
else to make it look intentional. When that didn't
work, she ran to the bathroom for a cloth and some
water to scrub the blob away. Instead, the paint only
smeared and the spot grew. Then she got some dry
paper towels and tried to soak up the bigger, wetter
smear and rub it off, but by now she had rubbed a big
hole in her paper. She was in tears.

Finally, she brought the drippy, pitiful mess to where
I was working and held it up to me. Her little chin
quivered and the tears dripped onto the already soggy
paper as she sobbed, "Oh, mommy, I wanted so much

to make you something beautiful, but now look: it's all a mess, and I can't fix it!" I stooped down and gathered her up into my arms. "I know. It's all right," I said. "Wait here." I went to the craft cupboard and brought out a brand-new sheet of manila paper. Her eyes danced when she saw it, and soon she was back at her little table singing as she started again to make what she'd had in mind.

Like little Suzanne, most of us begin with noble dreams and high aspirations. We're not going to mess up like others have done, we think. We're not going to make the mistakes our parents made or waste opportunities as our friends have done. But time marches by and life is so "daily." At first the blunders we make or the opportunities we miss don't seem so important. We think, "Aw, I'll fix that. I'll do it better next time." And maybe we try. We patch and fix, cover up and improvise, until one day we wake up to realize our lives are half gone and the dreams we had in the beginning are no closer to being realized than they were at the start. More and more we've settled for second best and status quo. And when we look back we see that we weren't real decision makers, but more often the victims of someone else's plan, and life isn't at all as we wanted it to be.

Now let me shout or whisper or sing the words once more: *we can start again*. Like Suzanne with her painting, we can take whatever mess we've made of life to the Father and say, "Here, Lord. I wanted to make something beautiful of my life. Take what is left of it." And He will take it, and if you let Him, He will make something beautiful of it all.

If there ever were dreams that were lofty and
   noble,
They were my dreams at the start;
And the hopes for life's best were the hopes that I
   harbored

Down deep in my heart;
But my dreams turned to ashes, my castles all
  crumbled,
My fortune turned to loss,
So I wrapped it all in the rags of my life,
And laid it at the cross.

Something beautiful, something good;
All my confusion, He understood;
All I had to offer Him was brokenness and strife,
But He made something beautiful of my life.[2]

"But if . . ."—Jesus knows about our broken dreams.
"But if . . ."—He's made a way.
"But if . . ."—There's a brand new sheet, a fresh
start, a new beginning.

In big theological terms, that is called *redemption*, a
word that simply means "being bought back." When
we sold ourselves short, Jesus bought us back; He died
to give us a brand new beginning, not just to patch us
up so that we could hobble along and drag ourselves
to the finish line and be accepted into some far-out-
there eternal utopia. No, Jesus died to let us start all
new, here and now, with no track record to be
ashamed of.

Forgiveness.

Re-creation.

New birth.

"But if . . ."

Those aren't some dusty, remote, theoretical terms!
They are real and personal, *and they mean that no matter
what our past has been we can start again,* as if the decisions
we make tomorrow are the first ones we've ever
made!

You may have heard that "people don't change."
Yes, they do. They may not change themselves on
their own, but when Christ comes to possess a person
who is totally submitted to Him, that person changes.

DECISION VISION

Letters come into our office daily from persons whose lives were ruined by unfortunate choices. They often tell of the disappointing results of efforts to reform themselves. Only a real awareness of God's transforming love and a childlike acceptance of His forgiveness were able to really change their lives.

After one of the Praise Gatherings in Indianapolis, a young woman from Illinois wrote:

> I have had a terrible past haunting me for years. My self-esteem was so low that it was nonexistent. I felt I had to apologize to the ground for walking on it. I had so much hatred and self-loathing that I would sit and cut myself with razor blades, just trying to punish myself. I was determined to destroy myself by running my husband away and giving up my two-year-old child. I was sure God hated me, too.
>
> We have lost three babies, and our church family prayed solidly for nine months and prayed our healthy, beautiful daughter into this world, but still in my twisted thinking, I could only see her as punishment from God and a reminder that I really should have a retarded, brain-damaged child to care for and not this exceptionally bright child that He gave me.
>
> I have lived on Valium for years. And I must admit that I much misused the drug. I could feel that I was being sucked down a big drain with no help in sight. I had tried psychiatrists, psychologists, and much counseling with my pastor and his wife. But I only continued to hate and destroy.
>
> I guess God had to send me to Indianapolis for three days until I finally felt His love sink in and become a reality for me. Intellectually,

I knew that God loved me, but for the first time in my whole life I finally could feel that He loved me. What joy! I bought a tape on "Loving Yourself," and I periodically played it over when I am tempted to return to the old self-punishing and hating habits. For the first time in my life I am glad to be alive and I do not want to die. I am happy and thankful my suicide attempts failed. I can even love me! Most of all, I can love other people instead of hiding from them. Before, I could not stand for anyone to touch me. Now I can put my arms around people and tell them I love them.

I have not had Valium in two months and experienced no problems dropping them so suddenly as I had been warned that I would. God is my tranquilizer now. What a difference it has made knowing that I AM LOVED! Recently my daughter's Sunday school teacher told me what a change she has been able to see in my daughter over these past weeks. I weep with joy. Because He loves me, I can love me and I can love my child.

And from Ohio a young father writes:

It was little more than a month ago when I felt as though my life on this earth were over. My wife had announced that she was leaving me (it was no real surprise, because she hasn't shown any love for me in years), temptation was all around me in the form of alcohol and women. I was depressed, rejected, and fed up with living. I was saved when I was a young boy, but God seemed so distant . . . so removed from my life. As a last resort (my final grasp for life) I called an old friend. . . . It was the spirit of God working through him that evening. Everything he said seemed to stab at my heart. My old nature was struggling for its life. But this was one battle that Satan was not going to win.

It was with the words of my two-year-old son (said as a prayer of thanks for a meal) and a simple slogan of a local church that the Lord once again took first place in my life.

My son's statement . . .

"Thank you, Jesus . . . for the cross!"

The slogan . . .

"You are loved!"

Such simple statements, but, oh, what meaning they carry to a soul in need of cleansing. I thank God for those words of life, of love. . . . they have made all the difference in my life!

It is not uncommon for people who have experienced pain and brokenness to confess that they have contemplated suicide. As Carl Sandburg asked, "Who can live without hope?" But hope is looking forward to that which lies ahead, and looking toward it with optimism. Hope is not possible when the past has our full attention and when that past is so disappointing that it gives us no reason to believe life could get better.

Only when the past, however tragic, is forgiven and wiped away by a love that is bigger than all our past sins, a love so grand that it does not turn its face away from any of our ugliness—only then can we dare to hope and believe again.

A young mother from Florida writes:

As a kid in high school and college I thought Christians were dull and lifeless creatures, so I became a young adult confident that I was the "master of my fate" and the "captain of my soul." Then came a broken marriage, and I was left with a tangled mess of a life and two little sons whom I merely tolerated most of the time.

Seven more years of one man after another went by—and then our Lord brought me to my knees after I seriously contemplated murder and suicide. In a tiny Baptist church where I grudgingly took my boys for a children's program, our patient heavenly Father claimed his lost children. He had waited thirty-five years for me, when I had trouble waiting a minute for my children. So you see, when I sing "The King is Coming," I just have to change the last line to "Thank God, He *waited* for me!"

Now all three of us DO "get excited and tell everybody" about our wonderful new relationship with Christ because, finally and forever, "we are loved." We're looking forward to spending eternity with you and your music, since we've just discovered you this Christmas, and we've missed a lot!

"Looking forward." A life-changing encounter with Jesus leaves each of us "looking forward." The following is from a letter we received from our friend Ruth Bell Graham. A minister from Asheville, North Carolina, had related to her a story that he'd discovered while visiting the Brushy Mountain Prison in Tennessee. Ruth writes:

There was in the Brushy Mountain Prison a prisoner by the nickname of "Big Red." He was the meanest, toughest, most incorrigible prisoner there. He had been there for seventeen years. Every new prisoner who arrived was frisked down and robbed by Big Red. All the other prisoners stood in awe of him.

Before the days when flogging prisoners

was outlawed, Big Red was frequently subjected to brutal beatings by the guards with leather straps. During each ordeal Big Red never broke down; he only cursed the guards.

But Big Red had one weakness: he was hooked on heroin. One day, needing a fix, he sent for the prisoner who was the supplier. The guy gave him a shot of heroin and then demanded his forty dollars in payment. Big Red's reply was, "Try and get it!"

The supplier kept his cool and bided his time. The next time Big Red ordered a fix, the supplier produced a syringe, which Big Red held up to the light and then grinned with pleasure because he realized that there was twice the normal amount in the syringe.

No sooner had he received the injection when Big Red went into violent convulsions. The supplier had filled the syringe with half heroin and half lighter fluid. The previous prisoner who had received such a dose had died in excruciating agony. But the medics got to Big Red in time and, partly due to his good health and tremendous physique, combined with the medical attention that he received, Big Red pulled through.

Once more he was thrown into solitary confinement. Here he lay face down on his cot, and for the first time in his life wave after wave of loneliness swept over him. He had never felt such desolation before. In order to counteract it, he reached up and put a cassette in his little cassette player, hoping that the rock-and-roll would help lift his spirits.

Instead of the expected rock-and-roll, he heard someone singing "He Touched Me." For some strange reason, he was caught by

the words and listened. Over and over he
played it, and as he did, the tears that never
came when he was being flogged began to
flow. He lay face down on his cot, racked
with sobs, while Connie Smith, the country-
and-western star, sang "He Touched Me."
There in his tiny cell, Big Red realized the
love of God in Christ Jesus and, asking for
mercy, he received it and asked the Lord
Jesus into his heart.

Such a remarkable change came to his life
in the next few days that the other prisoners
viewed him with suspicion. Even the warden
was suspicious. He called Big Red into his
office and demanded what he was up to. Big
Red, with tears in his eyes, told him exactly
what had happened. From somewhere he got
a Bible, which he carried under his arm at all
times, and he goes around the prison fear-
lessly witnessing to the other prisoners concerning the power of the Lord Jesus to forgive
sins and change a man. A number of prisoners
have been converted, and the rest don't dare
argue with him.

And from Los Angeles County jail Bill and I received
a quite different story:

I am in the Los Angeles County jail. Now
that could be the beginning of a sad story,
but my story is wonderful since it has an
ending so grand and glorious I can hardly
maintain my writing calm.

At the age of twelve I was called to preach
in a dream, in which a tiny child asked me,
"Who is God?" For the next fourteen years I
tried to suppress all thoughts of that dream
and its implications. My goals were much too

important. I knew I had a grand future in politics.

By the age of twenty-four I had been appointed by the Nixon Administration to a Presidential Advisory Council, counted a former President as a friend, was listed in most political "who's who" volumes, had known most of the great and near great in our government.

"If there ever were dreams that were lofty and noble"— In 1974 I was a candidate for State Representative, district two, of Texas. In the runoff I lost by only nine hundred votes and the press predicted a bright future of this twenty-four year old. For years then my only religion was politics, and my "gods" were politicians. I loved Richard Nixon beyond words and worshiped him literally.

Following my political loss and the downfall of Nixon that same summer, I began the descent deeper into sin and then later into crime.

On May 20, 1977, I was arrested for the theft of rare political documents from UCLA. and the state of Texas. In August I was sentenced to a year in county jail, where I've been since.

After a month here I was led almost to committing suicide. On the night I planned this last act of sin I opened my Bible at random and what I saw I could not believe. I asked Christ into my heart and turned my life over to Him—I had done nothing constructive with my life thus far. I accepted Christ's call to preach and will enter seminary when I am released later this summer.

The miracle of the new! A chance to start again! "As

far as the east is from the west," He has removed our sins from us, and buried them in the deepest of the seas.

But beginning again can be scary. Starting anew means facing responsibility. Acknowledging our failures and accepting God's wonderful forgiveness also entails *forsaking* our past and going on to an exciting but unknown future. Total healing of our broken past requires that we begin to do something to construct a new life.

I have always been intrigued by Jesus' statement to the crippled man near the pool of Bethesda, "Do you want to get well?" (see John 5:6, NIV). On the surface, that sounds like a stupid question. "Of course he wants to be well!" I would probably have said had I been there. "He's been lying here, helpless for thirty-eight years, totally dependent on the others to feed him, clothe him, carry him from place to place. Why, he can't even help himself to the edge of the therapeutic waters when they are troubled. Then you ask if he wants to be well. Anyone in his right mind wants to be well!"

But Jesus knew human nature. He knew the way we cling to the familiar, even when it is painful, to avoid the risk of the unknown. He knew how frightening it can be to face responsibility. He was, no doubt, asking the man, "Are you ready to begin living as a whole person? Are you willing to take the responsibility of making and following through on your own decisions instead of letting others decide for you? Are you ready to live without excuses, to have no one or nothing but yourself to blame for the direction of your life? *Do you want to be well?*" It was a good question.

It is also a question we each must answer, for forgiveness and redemption are only the beginning. Forsaking the past demands that we move toward and deal with the future. The decision to become a "new creature" is the first in a whole lifetime of new choices that have to be made. "Forgetting what is behind" is only the beginning. The greatest amount of energy is required for the rest of the task, that of "straining toward what is ahead" and "pressing on toward the goal."

Abraham Maslow in his book *Toward a Psychology of Being* writes:

> Growth has not only rewards and pleasures but also many intrinsic pains and always will have. Each step forward is a step into the unfamiliar and is possibly dangerous. It also means giving up something familiar and good and satisfying. It frequently means parting and a separation, ever a kind of death prior to rebirth, with consequent nostalgia, fear, loneliness, and mourning. It also means giving up a simpler and easier and less effortful life, in exchange for a more demanding, more responsible, more difficult life. Growth forward is in spite of these losses and therefore requires courage, will, choice, and strength in the individual, as well as protection, permission, and encouragement.[3]

When our lives are devastated by bad choices, we tend to want to give up, to sit down and quit—even to do away with ourselves. When we experience conversion and come to know the healing of forgiveness, we may feel as if we have arrived. That is the time, however, that we must face the task of working with the Holy Spirit to chart a new course and face an exciting, if sometimes frightening, new path.

When I was a child, a tornado hit the little village where we lived, and the house of a family we knew was damaged. One wall of the house exploded outward and was carried away by the wind, leaving the living room exposed like a room in a cut-away model. The furniture was blown about and there was some rain damage, but the family did not abandon their home. The first thing they did was to protect the exposed room by covering the end of the house with several layers of strong plastic. They called in a builder to assess the damage and notified the insurance company.

Next, they needed to decide whether the wall should be replaced exactly as it was or if this was a good time to improve the structure. The materials were ordered and finally the house was restored.

When the storms of our lives come, the damage sometimes seems so bad that there is just no use going on. We are tempted just to give up or check out. But if we will call in the Master Builder and commit to work patiently through the problems and build anew, in time we can see our lives whole again.

A very special young friend of mine wrote the following true story in her own words. Only the names have been changed.

I am twenty-two years old, married to a guy, twenty-eight, whom I am crazy about and—the nice thing about that—who is crazy about me. We have two beautiful daughters ages five and nine months. We live in a great little town like a million others in the United States. We have a nice home, a compact car, and an old truck on its last leg. I stay home while my husband goes off to work five days a week. Some days the most exciting event is fishing the baby out of the toilet or trying to entertain a five-year-old who is absolutely sure there is nothing to do! I know this is a typical day in the lives of millions of other young women, but when I look back from where the Lord has brought me, the story gets less and less typical.

At sixteen I was a young Christian from a

terrific family, but at such a tender age, I was a victim of bad choices—my own! I had just finished my tenth year of high school and was on summer break when I met Ken for the first time at a party. He was six years older and had just dropped out of college. Right away I knew he was special. We started to date, and though I had never had a sexual relationship before and as a Christian knew that it should be saved for marriage, when we were together I somehow forgot all I knew. In two months I was pregnant.

I felt as if it were the end of the world. Mentally, I was sick, and my self-esteem hit rock bottom. I felt I had let down my folks. I knew how much they had struggled in their own lives so that they could do more for us kids. I dreaded telling them so much that I kept my pregnancy a secret for five months, reading medical books over and over for symptoms, trying to tell myself I didn't have any.

Not telling anyone left me feeling alone and abandoned without direction—like I was stuck. The love I had felt for Ken turned to a sort of hate. I don't know how you can feel both, but I did. I had become something I hated, and I felt it was his fault: he could walk away and nobody would know he was pregnant; he wouldn't soon be putting on forty pounds!

Right away I was faced with some really big decisions:

1. *Marriage.* I didn't have to think about it long to know that that wasn't in anybody's best interest. I was so young and Ken and I were both so confused that I knew marriage wouldn't work for us. So Ken left for the

service later in the summer and I carried the burden alone.

2. *Telling my parents.* As I said, I thought about this for five months before I could face the hurt I knew I'd see in their eyes and the disappointment in me I knew they'd feel. But I knew, too, that they were the two people in the world who loved me most, and I desperately needed guidance and knew it had to come from someone who knew life and loved me. I decided I couldn't seek help from someone who didn't know any more than I did. To tell them was a hard but good decision. It seemed that for a week we did nothing but talk and cry and pray. At first they felt guilty, too, and it tore me up to sense that they were accusing themselves, wondering if they'd loved me enough, taught me enough, failed me in some way. But after a while the awful burden of it all seemed to lift, and they said, "Okay, we will go on." During this time there were Christian friends and my brothers, too, who sort of took turns helping me bear the load. The Lord hadn't left me after all! He was all around me.

3. *What was to be done about the baby?* At first all the thoughts ran through my mind: abortion, giving up the baby for adoption, keeping the baby and becoming a young, very young, single parent. For me, abortion was out of the question. This was a real life growing inside of me. I decided to keep the baby, and my parents, who gave me the freedom to make my choice, also assured me of their love and support. We decided I would live at home and work to raise my child. In the spring I had a precious baby girl (8 lbs., 10 oz.). Dad stayed with me in the labor room and was

just great! Mother, just outside, was going through every pain with me.

That fall I went back to finish high school. Many of the same kids who most pressured me to believe that sex was what everyone did dropped me cold and treated me like a leper. But in spite of some rough times I graduated with my class and worked as a secretary and receptionist for the next two years.

In the meantime, Ken had done a lot of searching. I know the Lord was dealing with him all along. Two-and-a-half years after my baby was born, we were married, now as two matured adults. Since we've been married, he's become a Christian. We're still struggling through life's everyday situations, but we're growing and loving and the Lord is making something out of what seemed, five years ago, to be hopeless.

God can make something beautiful out of what each of us thought was hopeless. When I look at my life, I, too, sometimes get discouraged with my progress. I feel that I am pitifully inadequate for any of the tasks that lie ahead. Some days I am disappointed with myself as a mother and wife. I get frustrated with the trouble I have budgeting my time and producing the work I know I could be capable of doing. I get downright embarrassed about my musical abilities.

Your story is, perhaps, different from any of these. But whatever is in your past, God wants to help you leave it behind (except for what you might learn from it) and go on. Dwelling on the past—successes or failures—is a waste of energy and a sin against the Holy Spirit, whose work is to call out the gifts we have and make of us all God wants us to be. Even failure can be the springboard to growth and discovery, so we should never allow the fear of it to keep us from daring to risk.

Part of life's great adventure is the growth process itself. There is wonderful freedom and joy in coming to recognize that the fun is in the becoming. As long as we live, we will never "arrive," but only discover new tracts of unexplored territory.

> I am learning to trust in the process
> Of what Jesus is doing to me;
> Since I made Him Lord, I believe His Word—
> There's no end to all the things I could be.
>
> I am lying back in the promise
> That He's working in it all for my good;
> Oh, I'm not what I want to be,
> But thank God, I'm not what I was.
>
> Doing always goes with believing,
> Believing comes when I obey;
> If I take the risk and just follow;
> He'll be there to show me the way.
>
> Oh, I'm not what I want to be,
> I'm not what I'm gonna be,
> But, thank God, I'm not what I was.[4]

Behind us all is the past; before us is the future. For some, the past is full of pain and mistakes. Others may be intimidated by the accomplishments of the past or tempted to gloat over past achievements or rest on past laurels. But we all have a choice. We can be paralyzed by the past and terrified of the future. Or we can learn from our mistakes, be forgiven for our blunders, put our past accomplishments in perspective, and use what we have learned to be bigger more tender, more loving people.

To all decision makers come these words of power concerning the past:

All these things that I once thought very
worthwhile—now I've thrown them all away
so that I can put my trust and hope in Christ
alone. Yes, everything else is worthless when
compared with the priceless gain of knowing
Christ Jesus my Lord (Phil. 3:7-8).

I repent for hours I have spent
Recalling all the pain and failures of my past;
And I repent for dwelling on the things
Beyond my power to change
The chains that held me fast.

I give up the bitterness and hate,
The blaming men and fate for all my discontent;
The guilt and pain I empty from my cup,
So God can fill it up
With peace and sweet content.

I accept the promise of the dawn,
A place to build upon to make a brand new day.
I will begin convinced that Jesus lives
Assured that He forgives
And that He's here to stay.

I will go on! My past I leave behind me.
I gladly take His mercy and love.
He is joy and He is peace;
He is strength and sweet release.
I know He is and I am His.
I will go on![5]

FOR WORK AND DISCUSSION

1. A helpful little prayer goes like this: "God, give us grace
   to accept with serenity the things that cannot be
   changed, courage to change the things which can be
   changed, and the wisdom to distinguish the one from
   the other."[6] In your mind or on paper, list the things in

your life that fall into these two categories:

Things I cannot change	Things I can change
about the past	about my circumstances
about present circumstances	about myself
	about my relationships to others

2. How much energy are you wasting on things you cannot change? On regret? On worry? On fear of what might happen in the future? Study Philippians 4:6, 1 Peter 5:7, Luke 12:29 (the *Living Bible* paraphrase may be helpful).

3. What percentage of your time and thought processes are you devoting to positive decision making and problem solving? What percentage of your daily conversation is devoted to "going forward"; how much is given to pessimism, negative comments, and "looking back"?

4. If someone gave you a beautiful gift, you would think it rude to reject or belittle it. God's forgiveness is His free gift, bought at a great price. What are some ways to reject or belittle His gift? How can we live out our acceptance of His Gift?

5. How are we sometimes guilty of keeping others from accepting God's gift of forgiveness for their posts?

6. Read once more Philippians 3:7-14. What does it mean to press "toward the mark for the prize of the high calling of God in Christ Jesus?" This is the opposite of status seeking or social climbing. Why? How does "pressing toward the mark" affect the way we make decisions in regard to other believers? Unbelievers?

7. How does "forgetting those things which are behind" and the awareness of God's forgiveness affect

our self-confidence? Our ability to function as decision makers?

1. Reuben Welch, *We Really Do Need Each Other*. ©1973 by Impact Books. All rights reserved. Reprinted by permission of The Benson Company, Inc., Nashville.
2. "Something Beautiful," lyrics by Gloria Gaither, ©1971 by William J. Gaither.
3. Abraham H. Maslow, *Toward a Psychology of Being*, 2nd ed. (New York: Van Nostrand Reinhold Company, Div. of Litton Educational Publishing, 1968), 204.
4. "I'm Not What I Want to Be," lyric by Gloria Gaither, ©1978 by William J. Gaither.
5. "I Will Go On" lyric by Gloria Gaither, ©1978 by William J. Gaither.
6. John Bartlett, ed., *Familiar Quotations* (Boston: Little, Brown and Company, 1980), 823.

Prayer for
Decision Makers

O Father of Wisdom,
My life is filled with decisions and choices that constantly strain to the limit my abilities to reason and think and make judgments. I know that I am not equal to the task of living and making a difference in this crazy world. I am surrounded in every area of my life, nearly every waking moment, with values and voices that contradict God's Word. Help me to stay close to the Word so that I may know You—really know You. Bring into my life people who also know You, who love me enough to be my most honest critics. Help me to resist the temptation to surround myself with people who simply feed my ego and who tell me only what they know I want to hear.

I commit myself to be Your person in my world, asking to be not of this world, but to make a difference as I stay and work and think and make decisions in it—decisions that could change it—for Your sake.

Forgive me, Lord, for wasting any of Your precious gifts of energy or time by mulling over the failures or glories of my past. May I begin this moment to press toward the high calling for me in Christ Jesus.

Amen.

Suggested Additional Reading

Benson, Bob. *See You at the House*. Nashville: Thomas Nelson, 1989.

Conway, Jim. *Adult Children of Legal or Emotional Divorce*. Downers Grove, Ill: InterVarsity Press, 1990.

Dobson, James. *Parenting Isn't for Cowards*. Waco, Tex: Word, 1990.

Dobson, James and Gary Bauer. *Children at Risk*. Waco, Tex: Word, 1990.

Foster, Richard J. *Celebration of Discipline: The Path to Spiritual Growth*. San Francisco: Harper & Row, 1978. Rev. ed. 1988.

Gaither, Gloria. *What My Parents Did Right*. Nashville: Star Song Publishers, 1991.

Hart, Archibald D. *Overcoming Anxiety*. Waco, Tex: Word, 1989.

Lawrence, Brother. *The Practice of the Presence of God*. Old Tappan, NJ: Fleming H. Revell Co., 1958.

Lucado, Max. *Six Hours One Friday*. Portland, Ore: Multnomah Pr., 1989.

Manning, Brennan. *The Ragmuffin Gospel*, Portland, Ore: Multnomah Pr., 1990.

Miller, Holly and Dennis Hensley. *How to Stop Living for the Applause*. Ann Arbor, Mich: Servant, 1990.

Nouwen, Henri J. M. *In the Name of Jesus*. New York: Crossroad, 1989.

O'Connor, Elizabeth. *Eighth Day of Creation: Gifts and Creativity*. Waco, Tex: Word, 1971.

Peterson, Eugene H. *A Long Obedience in the Same Direction.* Downers Grove, Ill: InterVarsity, 1980.

Porat, Friedan. *Creative Procrastination: Organizing Your Own Life.* New York: Harper & Row, 1980.

Powell, John. *Fully Human, Fully Alive.* Allen, Tex: Argus Communications, 1976.

Seamands, David. *Living With Your Dreams.* Wheaton, Ill: Scripture Press, 1990.

Sheehy, Gail. *Pathfinders.* New York: William Morrow, 1981.

Shelly, Marshall. *Keeping Your Kids Christian.* Ann Arbor, Mich: Servant, 1990.

Smalley, Gary, and John Trent. *Two Sides of Love.* Waco, Tex: Word, 1990.

Tada, Joni Eareckson. *Glorious Intruder,* Portland, Ore: Multnomah Pr., 1989.

Tournier, Paul. *The Meaning of Persons.* New York: Harper & Row, 1957.

Trueblood, Elton. *A Place to Stand.* New York: Harper & Row, 1969.

Welch, Reuben. *We Really Do Need Each Other.* Nashville: Impact Books, 1974.

About the Author:

GLORIA GAITHER's occupation might be listed as wife-mother-lyricist-author-speaker-recording artist and performer. Since graduation from college and her marriage to noted songwriter-business entrepreneur Bill Gaither in 1962, Gloria has written ten books and many articles for leading Christian and secular publications. She coauthored 10 major musicals (including the award-winning *Alleluia*), and has been the lyricist for more than five hundred songs many of which have became standards in Christian music around the world.

Although she gives top priority to her marriage, the lives of her three grown children (Suzanne, Amy, and Benjy), and her writing, Gloria travels extensively as a speaker and as one-third of the internationally acclaimed Bill Gaither Trio, winner of two Grammy Awards, ten Dove Awards. They have recorded more than forty albums with sales of more than four million. Gloria received the Dove award in 1984 for "Song of the Year" for "Upon this Rock," co-written by Dony McGuire.

Gloria has received honorary doctorates from four colleges and universities. In 1991, she finished her Master of Arts Degree in English Literature and is currently continuing graduate studies at Ball State University. She also teaches part-time at Anderson University, her alma mater.